Courageous World Catalysts II

11 Inspirational Stories by Changemakers on their Missions for Global Impact

Copyright © 2018 Vickie Gould International, LLC All rights reserved.

This book or parts thereof may not be reproduced in any form, stored in any retrieval system, or transmitted in any form by any means—electronic, mechanical, photocopy, recording, or otherwise—without prior written permission of the authors or publisher, except as provided by United States of America copyright law.

This anthology project was led and compiled by Vickie Gould, Law of Attraction Business and Book Coach. www.vickiegould.com email vickie@vickiegould.com

Cover by: Michael Corvin

Edited by: Andrea McCurry

Co-authored by

- **Vickie Gould** - Law of Attraction Business and Book Coach

- **Jay Diamond** - Pleasure and Intimacy Coach, Best Selling Author, Speaker

- **Sally Dibden** - Founder of The Wellbeing Consultants, Holistic Health & Life Coach, Physiotherapist

- **Lori Granito** - Business Mentor and Strategist, Success Coach, 4 x TEDx Speaker, Founder of Legendary Coaching and the Boss Lady Millionaires Club

- **Angela Irwin** - Life Coach, TEDx Speaker, Founder of Joyful Life Solutions

- **Dijana Jovanoska, PhD** - Business Consultant, Personal Coach, Author

- **Lisa Nielsen**, Benefit Specialist and Educator

- **Jane Richardson, PhD** - Communication Consultant, Expert Witness & Author

- **Merav Richter** - Vivacious Shero for Brave Ecstatic Living. Author, Performer, Advocate

- **Brandi Stephens** - Resiliency Coach, Speaker, Educator

- **Beverly Walthour** – TV & Radio Show Host, Business Strategist, Speaker, and Author

Want to be in the next anthology?

Do you dream of one day becoming a published author? Do you want to make your mark and have a lasting impact? Do you know that there are people out there waiting on your message – to hear your exact story?

Then, I'd like to invite you to participate in the next anthology and become a Best Seller like the authors in this anthology.

All you have to do is turn in your story and I'm going to give you easy-to-follow steps to writing it so that it speaks to those people who need your help. I'm also going to take away the tech overwhelm by publishing the book for you and guaranteeing the Best Seller status. Plus, I'm even going to have your story professionally edited.

Go here for details on the next project – join or get on the waiting list: http://bit.ly/nextanthology

Acknowledgement

Every time I put together an anthology, I never know what stories I'll get. I'm consistently blown away with the tenacity, perseverance and character of the authors that are in my compilations. It is their vulnerable moments and raw truths that truly make this book a living legacy. Thank you to all the authors for another amazing anthology!

Special thanks to Andrea McCurry for her fabulous job editing everyone's stories. This could not have been created without your huge support!

Table of Contents

Acknowledgement 9

Jello Fluff and Extra-Long Hugs – That's What Legacies are Made Of by Vickie Gould 13

Can You Let Go of a Dream to Receive a Life Purpose? by Jay Diamond 20

A Perfectly Imperfect French Dream by Sally Dibden 33

Just Keep Swimming by Lori Granito 46

Full Circle by Angela Irwin 56

Be a Success Story by Dijana Jovanoska 66

The Basketball Game by Lisa Nielsen 80

The Most Important Skill & Secret to Success by Jane Richardson 92

Nowhere Spells Now Here by Merav Richter 104

The Grit Factor by Brandi Stephens 114

It's Time to Take That Leap With FAITH! by Beverly Walthour 122

Jello Fluff and Extra-Long Hugs – That's What Legacies are Made Of

By Vickie Gould

I couldn't believe what I was hearing. My husband told me over the phone, "He's gone. It happened in his sleep." I heard how knotted up his voice was, and I froze for a split second.

Nah, it wasn't true. My brain wasn't willing to believe it.

Just a few hours earlier, my husband called saying he couldn't get a hold of his dad. They texted every morning since his mom passed because Dad lived alone. I told my husband that Dad was probably out, maybe at the doctor's office where the buildings have thick walls, and the reception is sometimes horrible.

My mind wanted to believe my story – that he was just out around town like normal. He was an active 80-year old man. Sharp as a tack, always cracking a joke, and he knew everyone. He was loved by everyone.

We joked that he went out for walks around his small neighborhood because he was canvassing for votes to be on the association board. The other place he was always at was church. He was there two or three times a week, doing the books, helping out anywhere that was needed, and mentoring the teens.

So, it couldn't be true. He was too spry. He hadn't been sick.

As I drove the hour and 15 minutes to his house to be with my husband, I ran through all the scenarios in my head of what could've happened. I cried and called my dad on the way to ask him what needed to be done first. We were in charge of the estate and trust. What should we do now?

When I got there, the police had already come and gone. We sat and waited for the coroner, and the rest was a blur. In fact, the next couple weeks were a blur as we got my husband's siblings together, cleaned and cleared out the house, set up an estate bank account, got three different stories from the probate court about what information we needed, found keys for the safe deposit box, and called everyone who needed to know. Plus, we planned the funeral, which was just 11 days later.

I answered the questions over and over again, "What happened?" We suspected the previously sweltering days had contributed to his death. Dad didn't like to have to use the bathroom too often, so he didn't drink on hot days, and it had been a hot week. He had been out gardening the night before.

His sudden death just didn't make sense. Could it have been such a simple thing as drinking water? If so, I was a little mad at him for cutting our time with him short. On the other hand, I realized that God knew this was his day.

And Dad got what he wanted – not to burden his children with illness, not to have to deal with dementia like some of his siblings had, and to be able to enjoy his every last day here on earth.

During this time, the one thing I was thankful for was owning my own business. I could re-arrange my schedule and take my calls from any location. My husband took bereavement leave from his corporate job. They gave him a measly three days.

I tried to be strong for my husband. I tried to concentrate on work. I tried to keep busy (something I'm actually really good at). I tried to not think too much about his being gone or I'd cry. I pushed off some appointments but I knew I couldn't reschedule them twice, though I wanted to. I didn't mind the work I had to do, but I didn't feel like showing up socially anywhere or putting on a happy face.

The day I made Jello fluff was hard for me. Dad always made this highly-requested dessert when we got together, and my husband thought the gesture would be a nice memory for when we threw my son's graduation party. The party had already been scheduled and happened to be two days before Dad's funeral. The thought of Dad not ever making Jello fluff again for us led me to sob and run up the stairs to cry on my husband's shoulder.

I thought that my prior health issues with chronic Lyme Disease had already made me evaluate my life fully. I decided back then that I didn't want to live a life of regrets. From that point on, I decided that I would no longer squelch who I wanted to be, that I would speak my mind more often, that I would stop putting myself last, and that I didn't want to look back ever again, lamenting the life I didn't live. Those realizations led me to open my business. I also decided to choose to be happier and work on letting go of the past. I no longer wanted to get angry, hold on to stupid stuff, or make things out to be a bigger deal than they had to be.

See, Dad made a huge impact. Pastor said that the whole church was grieving because he was such a big part of it. I heard that one of the teens he mentored was beside herself. There were two church members who postponed their vacations to be home for his funeral. In addition, one of the doctor's offices that I left a message for called me back to ask what happened and when the funeral was, so they could attend.

I heard stories from all of Dad's friends about the smiling, joking, happy man who brought joy everywhere he went. They said he gave the best hugs, and I knew that was true from experience. His hugs were extra-long, and they made you feel like he was sending extra love.

Dad's passing made me reevaluate my life again. What am I doing with my days? How will I be remembered? What kind of impact am I making on my kids? What does it matter who I touch in the world, if I don't make a big enough impact on my family?

My business has never been about the money. Sure, I want fun vacations and experiences for my family, or a pair of Valentino heels … or two. Mostly though, it is about making my mark on the world, being known for something important before I die. I want to have impact and create transformation in people's lives. I want them to see in themselves what they've never seen and to experience the possibilities they thought were reserved for other people. I want my clients to experience the life they didn't always believe they could have.

And now I'm left wondering if that's enough for me. It's not that I want a huge funeral. In fact, I told my family I don't want a funeral at all, but I want people to say similar things that they said about Dad – that I was a positive influence in their lives, that I always brought sunshine with me wherever I went, and that my hugs filled them up with lots of love.

I still can't believe that he's gone, and I won't be able to hug him again. I have a new recipe that I think Dad would love, but he'll never get to try it, and I saw something at the store the other day that made me think of him. Many times, I think of things I want to tell him, but I can't.

I'm glad I didn't erase his last voicemail to me, so I can replay it when I want a good laugh or just hear his voice. He had butt-dialed me and didn't know why my voicemail was talking to him, so he left a message anyway. Typical Dad. I had spoken to him since that message, but I still wish I could call him back one more time.

The family thought we would be planning his 80th birthday party. He outlived the age at which his five siblings passed, and I know he felt like he got some bonus time – and he was thankful for that. He was supposed to have knee surgery soon, so that he could keep going on his road trips. The next one would have been to revisit some childhood spots and go out to Colorado.

His Jello fluff and the memories of our time together are his legacy that, luckily, I get to keep in my heart forever. And if I close my eyes, I can imagine him right here giving me one of his extra-long hugs.

Vickie Gould is a certified Law of Attraction Business and Book Coach. She helps her clients go from blank page to Best Seller and beyond. As a result of working with her, Vickie's clients are able to help others struggling like they once did, make the impact that they want and leave a lasting legacy through their Best-Selling Books.

Vickie has four Best-Selling books of her own and she has been involved and mentioned in numerous of her clients Best-Selling books as well. Her greatest joy is in seeing their message come alive in WORDS.

She lives with her husband and three kids, along with her addiction to superhero shows on Netflix.

Visit her and get her free template "How to get the Book Out of Your Head and Onto Paper" at www.vickiegould.com

Instagram @vickiegould
Twitter @vickie_gould
Facebook @vickiegouldcoach
Linkedin @vickiegould

Can You Let Go of a Dream to Receive a Life Purpose?

By Jay Diamond

Early each morning I greeted the ocean with a smile. The sun gently warmed my face as I cycled towards the coffee shop where I worked to open for the day.

There had been no plans to move to Hawai'i; yet there I was, still on Big Island, two months later, living, learning, and... changing.

It was quite a shift from my life in the UK. I was a daytime radio host, juggling another part-time job, radio interviews, production meetings, and a healing practice on the side that kept me constantly busy.

I really wanted to make it in radio. After eight years I still loved music, I loved people, and I loved giving people something to smile about. For years, I wrote for magazines, interviewed new artists, DJ'd in clubs, and supported the local music scene. But over the previous six months, there had been some cash flow problems at the radio station. Changes in the available finances caused everyone to consider how much time they could offer in the working week to keep things afloat. It was becoming more and more difficult to balance my ever-stretched time and finances to make life work, and I was slowly falling out of love with the process.

On top of that, 12 months earlier, a family member had a major mental health breakdown, and the fall-out created distance between family members and triggered old wounds I thought I had put to rest.

Instead of an awful one-time event, the fall-out of that breakdown became years-long; fighting to get mental health support, taking four-hour round trips to psychiatric units, and trying to keep my own anxiety under control.

I was depleted mentally, physically, and spiritually.

I felt like a balloon with a slow leak. I noticed that I became overwhelmed easily, and felt like I could never catch up with all I had to manage. I was embarrassed that I had suddenly lost confidence in myself and made silly mistakes in my work that was previously easy to do. However, what really frightened me, was that I couldn't remember things well because of the stress.

After a series of powerful dreams, I developed an unusual obsession with Hawai'i. An irresistible magnetic pull lured me in, and I found myself booking a ticket for one. I intended to visit for ten days via San Francisco, but I was over-powered with the notion that I had to leave the house where I was staying and place my belongings in storage.

I had been considering a move, yet wanted to take my time and find the right place on my return from holiday. A rush to pack up my things and hand in my notice was not on the agenda! However, the feeling to place everything I owned in storage got stronger and stronger, until I felt suffocated at the thought of staying in that house.

A short holiday turned my life around when I was quickly offered a work exchange on arrival. I took extended leave from my radio and part-time jobs for this once-in-a-lifetime opportunity.

Stirring from the slumber

I could hear the lapping of the waves and the squeaking of glass as I cleaned the shop front, sipping on my new favourite beverage: a dirty chai. I knew something in me had changed.

For the first time, in a long time; I was really, really relaxed.

And happy.

The night before, I met a man who once worked with Walt Disney and spent most of his life with the rich and famous in LA. I told him my life and work predicaments.

He gently sat me down. He could see I was a clever, driven woman who had hit a wall in life, and was clueless about what to do next.

'You know," he said, "look at Madonna. Why do you think she has lasted so long? Every ten years she reinvents herself. She doesn't stay stagnant. She's not holding on to the past trying to be the same person as last decade. She moves on. And so can you."

I realised that I was so afraid of being seen as a failure – by myself and those around me – that I had held on to this role and dream of working in radio well past its sell-by date. I put so much time, energy, and money into this dream, I was afraid to let it go.

Sometimes, the only thing standing in the way of a glorious new future is the fear of letting go of the past.

As I cleaned the windows of the shop, I realised that if working in a coffee shop was all I ever did, and I am truly happy, then it is enough. There was freedom in not having to prove myself as 'successful' anymore. The constant drive to keep the dream alive had started to drain me rather than ignite me. Sighing with relief, I thought, "It's ok to change direction in life."

It was time to reinvent myself, and let go of an old dream.

I have been a spiritual healer since I was 18 years old, but I kept it on the side lines. I was much more interested in being a DJ! However, when I left Hawai'i to go back home to the UK, I left the radio job completely and started afresh.

I built a website for my work as a healer, and people began to visit me for all sorts of reasons. Stress, family problems, relationship issues, childhood abuse, health scares. I heard their many stories and often directed my clients towards helpful books to read, herbs to drink, or meditation to practice. It was beautiful to watch them transform inside and out.

As I held more healing workshops for women, it became apparent that they were crying out for support and a safe place to share their pain with other women. There were many stories of women who had been beaten, abused, or assaulted.

But there was one big problem.

Many people didn't truly understand my expertise. My clients arrived sporadically at my door via word of mouth. A friend would recommend they come and see me, often reporting, "If she can help me, she can help you."

I have years of training in numerous healing traditions; shamanism, tantra, yoga, Reiki, Vortex Healing, and more. And despite experiencing numerous spiritual visions and messages, I was a little reluctant to talk about my visits from Angels, Jesus, and the deity Ganesh, for fear of being judged as a little crazy.

Even so, I diligently began writing a book all about healing, in the hopes it would help people understand the one main thing I learned in my 20 years as a healer:

Everyone has the capacity to break the chains of the past and heal their heart, if they wish.

After 18 months of work, my book was rejected by a major publisher. Disheartened, I had to go back to the drawing board and decided to attend a conference in Atlanta with one of my mentors, Lisa Nichols. I needed guidance.

Awakening from a deep sleep

"What is it you know at your core?" Lisa asked. "What is it you know you're here to do but keep running away from?!"

The hair stood up on the back of my neck, as a sudden moan erupted from my belly. Tears streamed down my face; I felt she had singled me out to speak to my spirit.

"What do you *really* have to teach, but have been too scared to do?" She continued.

I started to sweat as my mind raced, because I didn't want to admit it. It was too hard, too scary, and confronted my deepest fears.

My heart knew the answer, but my mind wasn't ready: recovery from sexual abuse.

That's the whole real reason my healing journey began.

It's the reason I initiated into Reiki at only 18, why I immersed myself in personal development, read hundreds of books, and completed dozens of healing programmes.

The pain I carried in my heart was like a tub of bleach with a leaky hole that slowly dripped and burned over my relationships, my body image, and my confidence for most of my life.

The pain eroded my trust in men, yet I still tried to win their love, often over my self-respect. That slow leak made me feel unattractive and like there was something wrong with me. I just never felt good enough.

But with time, dedication, and healing I managed to turn my self-assurance around. Then, for years I went on to show others how they could also heal from sexual abuse via my private sessions. I just didn't talk about that work much publicly.

A wave of white hot fear took over my body.

I intuitively knew that if I embraced this path, there would be a price to pay – my comfort.

I would not be able to stay comfortable and fully lead people in this arena. Embracing this new path meant telling my story, and not just the successes, but the failures, the fears, and the secrets.

How could I be authentic without sharing the nights I cried myself to sleep after another failed relationship, the times I dug my nails into my body because I hated it, the constant fear of being abandoned. I was used to sharing my vulnerabilities and experiences in my one-to-one sessions. When needed, I did anything to help women get the sex and relationships they really desired. I was happy to let them know they were not alone in their dark times and feelings of shame. But on a more public level?

I wasn't ready for that.

What judgements would people make about me? I found people were much more comfortable having silly, flippant, or complaining conversations about sex; but mature, loving adult conversations? Not so much.

But perhaps, this lack of mature conversation was all the more reason to write the book.

If I wanted to *really* help the people I knew I could assist, I had to tell the stories that needed to be told, to blow the lid off shame and secrecy.

"But why does it have to be me?" I thought to myself.

The answer was clear. Deep down, I knew healing around sexuality was my path; I had just resisted it for a long time.

The truth is, my years of training in deep healing and coaching people to recover their greatness prepared me for this journey.

All that was waiting was for me to say yes, publicly, to the work I'd done secretly for years.

> *"Once you make a decision, the universe conspires to make it happen"*
>
> *-Ralph Waldo Emerson*

Within a week, I changed my website, made an announcement, and changed my book title to *Abuse to Abundance*. I outlined the new book in only ten minutes because I knew exactly what it took to help people.

This realization took root in my spirit: my story wasn't mine to hold onto. I had to use it to help others overcome abuse in their own lives.

Creating the dream

There was a part of me that always felt like I needed to take another course or get another qualification so I could prove I was good enough to really help people heal the hurt in their hearts. I wanted to be really ready before I announced my work in sexuality and recovery to the world.

It didn't matter that to me I had already used my healing abilities for many years with amazing results. There was a little part of me that still felt like an imposter.

Have you ever had big dreams you didn't feel quite worthy of? Dreams that are so big they're kinda scary?

What I discovered is, if you wait until you are 'ready,' you'll always be waiting. The path unfolds AS you walk along it, not before. You have to take the first step in faith, then the next part of the path reveals itself. Each step takes faith.

I believe that showing up in your life's purpose work is a spiritual path *in itself*. You are constantly called to look at the places inside yourself where you keep yourself small, where you hide your visibility, where you don't appreciate your own value.

And when you have your own business, there is no one else to hide behind. It is all on you. The only way to succeed is to take a stand for your own greatness and claim, "YES! I am enough! I can fulfil the dream God has put in my heart!"

It's scary, and the only way to succeed is to trust the struggle and trust the process. Stay centred in your heart with the end goal in mind. If I permitted myself to dwell on what others might think or to compare myself to others, I would never allow myself to help them on their journey to healing.

I had to trust the plan for my life and surrender to the bigger calling, even though it felt too big for little old me. This was a dream I had to grow into. You might call it God's plan, or a call from the universe, but deep in my heart – despite all the nerves and discomfort -- I knew that I had been equipped for this task.

Like many others before me, I thought I needed to get 'there' first and **then** show up in my life's purpose. To have all the money and children and marriage and the house by the ocean before I could really show up for my calling; like maybe this would prove my success and 'healing.'

But I had it the wrong way around. I had to **grow into** the woman I was meant to be by doing the work I was meant to do.

When you answer the call, doors will and do open.

During my life I experienced hard times, and they fostered compassion in my heart. I learned a humility that nurtured excellence in my delivery, and I had a belief from personal experience in a healing power that conquered any fear.

So, knees-knocking and teeth-chattering, I took the leap and created the dream. And the clients came; stuck singles came, troubled couples came. I delivered workshops, created online programmes, and completed one-to-one mentorships to give my clients the best results possible in love, sex, and healing.

I saw healing and restoration, saved marriages, and soaring confidence.

I saw pain transform to hope before my eyes.

And I never doubted again.

It's true that being a sex and relationship coach raises some eyebrows, but these days, I take it as an opportunity to educate and inspire others to go deeper on the path of the heart, instead of as a reason to hide.

Jay Diamond is a pleasure and intimacy coach and the author of the International Best Seller *Abuse to Abundance*. She helps stuck singles find their soul mate and struggling couples get juicy and reconnected again. Her coaching, online courses, and workshops help people stand on top of their story, not underneath it, for a more orgasmic life and soul-level success. She has a special interest in assisting abuse survivors to live an abundant life.

Jay has appeared in *Mind, Body Green, Spirit & Destiny* magazine, *Elephant Journal,* and *Kindred Spirit Magazine* and speaks internationally.

You can reach Jay at: www.jaydiamond.net

A Perfectly Imperfect French Dream
By Sally Dibden

"Your inner knowing is your only true compass."

– Joy Page

I fell in love with the French Alps at age 17, despite dismally failing French A-level. I remember dancing out of the exam hall thinking, "At least I'll never have to write a word of French again!"

It was thanks to that blip in my set of otherwise great grades, that I had to wait a whole year for a place at my preferred University. Initial disappointment turned to huge excitement as I opened my mind to other possibilities. Within a few weeks, I landed a dream gap-year job as an au pair, working for a couple who were ski instructors in La Plagne, France.

I loved the free spirit of this delightful young family and almost everyone I met in the 'mountain bubble.' People lived life on their terms – winter in the mountains, summer by the sea, travel, repeat. This lifestyle felt like truly living – pursuing what you really loved, rather than surviving in a rat race.

After spending that summer in the South of France, returning to Manchester University to pursue a generalized degree no longer felt exciting, nor necessary. By Christmas I quit; I had a new plan: apply to study Physiotherapy, then set up my practice in the Alps upon graduation. I returned to England

and embarked on what felt like this far more aligned route, and I was all set to head to France in the final year.

However, a serendipitous encounter during my last clinical placement, at the Royal Air Force Officer Training School in Lincolnshire, changed my course. I met Rich, a pilot and officer, at the reputed Summer Officer Graduation Ball. We danced until breakfast, and the rest is history.

After a whirlwind two-week romance, we headed off for a six-year posting to Scotland. It was beautiful there and provided the outdoors lifestyle we loved. We water-skied in the Moray Firth, ran across the rugged coastline, and cycled across the Highlands. We not only travelled frequently together, I negotiated a sabbatical from work to complete another ski season to satisfy my soul that snowboarding would be a hobby not an Olympic pursuit!

Shortly after my return from a round-the-world working trip, Mother Nature intervened, and I fell pregnant. I'm guessing we'd have found many projects and adventures to delay our primary soul's desire journey to have children, but after the initial surprise, Rich and I embraced the timing to get on with it.

Rich was reposted, and we were thankful to be near family in England for the first two years of utter chaos and bonding with our gorgeous baby boy. Yet, I still dreamt about bringing up our family overseas. After a few twists and turns, a wedding on the ski slopes, and a beautiful baby girl later — we got our chance. Rich left the Air Force and was offered a job as an airline pilot based in Switzerland. With two toddlers in tow, we were delighted to finally move to neighbouring France!

The first year or two of our new adventure were pretty much as I dreamed they would be. Winter in the French Alps and a seemingly endless summer by Lake Geneva. Plenty of outdoor fun, exploring with the children. New friendships, settling into school, and becoming part of the community.

Yet, it gradually became evident that raising a family away from your native country and language, without family support, also has its challenges. Rich's job responsibilities increased, and he was based away from home. Even though I made great friends, I felt like I was raising the children single-handedly.

> **"Pay attention to the whispers so you don't have to listen to the screams."**
>
> – Cherokee Proverb

The airline industry is tough, especially with young children. With relentless early starts and late finishes, Rich started to have a string of niggly injuries and illness — he was physically exhausted and emotionally depleted. Arguments increased between us. He seemed impatient and disconnected with the children's needs. I continued running the home, raising the kids, doing sports, building my physio practice, and staying sociable, but I felt isolated without Rich's support alongside.

It seemed our French Dream was falling apart. I was incredibly grateful for so much, yet several areas of my life were out of alignment.

- I was increasingly frustrated with the physiotherapy profession for which I'd had such high hopes and dreams. Despite having set up my own private practice, it was challenging in France — littered with restrictions and low pay.
- My father was unreliable, and it was increasingly clear to me that his dependency on alcohol played a significant role in this. It made communication particularly difficult. A destructive co-dependent triangle had been created between my separated parents and I, and sadly, my relationship with my mother deteriorated too.
- As if to refocus our attention, around this time, a close family member suddenly became ill after a seemingly insignificant accident. It was an immensely stressful period, involving relentless research for alternative therapies to complement the care we received through the health system.

We were catapulted into the world of nutritional therapy, naturopathy, and functional medicine to try and get to the root cause of the chronic condition.

After a turn for the worse, I suspect out of desperation, I discovered the skill of meditation. I heard whispers confirming my decisions and treatment guidance not to head to the hospital for a higher dose of medicine. The same evening, I also had an unusual urge to pray for healing. Miraculously, the next morning our dear family member was fine, went on to have no further symptoms, and made a full recovery.

An immense gratitude for health and life followed. A classic case of 'you don't know what you've got until it's gone.' I also realized my new-found meditation and prayer were incredibly powerful tools to use more often, not only in times of total crisis. They gave me strength and hope.

I do believe we're armed to cope when we must, to pull out all the reserves and do what we need to do. However, by the end of that intense year-long healing process, it became evident that my own health was far from optimal.

One evening whilst reaching for the biscuits, yet again, I realized just because I wasn't fat or overweight, didn't mean I was healthy. It suddenly dawned on me that I was both an emotional eater and sugar addict. I clearly didn't 'need' the biscuits nutritionally. Reaching for them crept in as a habit when I was stressed, upset, or alone. I was becoming one of those fit-looking sick people I'd seen in my practice time and time again!

I also really struggled to get up in the morning. Rich noticed mood changes and started tracking my monthly cycles so he could lie low during my monthly mood fluctuations! I was horrified that my dear body, which had always been incredibly strong and capable, seemed to be falling apart with an array of other symptoms such as anxiety, pelvic floor weakness, arm pain, hormonal headaches, and bloating.

By the time I sought help, my cortisol levels showed I was in adrenal fatigue — a condition often caused by chronic stress, leading to exhaustion, hormonal havoc, and burn-out. My holistic therapist was very clear on the cure: "Manage your stress levels, emotions, sleep, and sugar cravings, otherwise you will not get better."

> **"As you change the way you see the world, the world around you changes."**
>
> -- Wayne Dyer

I finally made a decision to prioritize my health and self. I knew my physical and emotional energy were key to our family dynamic. I became attuned to the stresses which triggered my decline. I extended my practice of techniques already familiar to me, such as mindfulness and the emotional freedom technique.

I radically increased my awareness and responsibility about my role in the dramas around me. I hired a therapist, read prolifically, and qualified as a holistic health coach. I became aware that I had been waiting for those around me, namely my parents and husband, to 'change.' I finally realized I couldn't expect anyone to change, except me.

However, I could learn to respond, not react. I could learn to release the anger and resentment which ate away at my precious energy reserves. I could get to the bottom of my emotional eating, hormone imbalances, and destructive habits. I could move forward professionally, so I didn't feel 'stuck.'

It was time to dream bigger. What was I born to do professionally? When you've been through certain personal experiences and seen enough patients and clients facing similar challenges, you notice the patterns. My patients responded dramatically to the more holistic treatment I began to offer them.

Time and time again, I witnessed patients and clients find that their blocks in body, life, and business were actually subconsciously held within suppressed negative emotions in their bodies. Their bodies or lives often became 'inflamed' in direct relation to these unprocessed emotions. Once accessed and released through a guided energy, shifting mindfulness process, I could often help them to completely dissipate these blocks, emotions, and symptoms.

Calming the thinking mind and listening to the body, I discovered, holds infinite wisdom around exactly who you are and what you *really* need for your life to be fulfilled, healthy, and happy.

I felt much more fulfilled and carved my path as a holistic health consultant, life and success coach, which meant I could work online with clients from all over the world. I realized that it was my zone of genius to empower driven achievers to heal, from not only the physical, but also the emotional stress-induced health issues, and rediscover balance and fulfillment in their busy lives.

I enrolled in a high-level, transformational, life-coaching program and spent three more years deepening my personal healing, solidifying my coaching skills, and learning how to build a business, as opposed to a hobby.

My relationships with my parents and husband gradually improved, in direct response to my ability to 'release' them from blame. The arm pain that had threatened my career disappeared as I dealt with resentment, the true origin of my physical pain. Forgiveness, it transpired, was the strongest medicine of all.

My hormones stabilized and pelvic floor strengthened, as I made changes with my sleep, food, exercise, and most importantly, my emotions. I started having better energy and tools for my kids and husband, as my capacity wasn't used up by my subconscious energy drains.

Meanwhile Rich started investing his energy into totally optimizing his health and fitness. He promptly manifested two job promotions within a year and our relationship, as well as his with the children, improved significantly.

> **"Heal yourself, change the world."** – *Carol Tuttle*

The wonderful side effect from healing ourselves is that everyone around us benefits! I feel so blessed to do the work I do. Whether I'm working with a CEO, a business owner, a teacher, or a parent, I know the effects will ripple out well beyond our work together.

It's clear that the issue of depletion and disconnection is far bigger than my personal observations and experience. In our results-orientated Western world, where accomplishments and speed are revered, our belief that we need to keep pushing, and insane pace of life are consistently fueled. All these aspects contribute to depleting and disconnecting from not only ourselves, but our environment, soils, fertility, and kids.

I passionately believe there is another way. There are many simple steps we can all take to experience our healthiest, happiest, most purposeful lives. Here are the primary three steps to check first:

1) Define what success means to you. Does it mean having the freedom to travel? Time with your kids? A certain salary? Having crystal clear clarity here will help you focus your time and attention, as well as make important decisions more easily.
2) Take time to stay connected with your desires, nature, and body. Gentle movement, such as walking or yoga, literally shifts stuck energy and emotions, creativity is unleashed, and solutions are found. This movement is all the more productive if this is outside in nature.
3) Slow down to speed up. Learn to be mindful, practice gratitude, and BE present. In this state we reconnect with our intuition and can hear the true voice of self or source inside.

The world needs smart men and women to heal and shine their light. Those who know when to stop pushing, to pause or ask for help, as opposed to leaping from crisis to crisis. Those who know when to release pain, guilt, perfection, or addiction, and simply listen to the voice inside to set them free.

These empowered warriors know to frequently reconnect: body, mind, and soul. They find a place from which they can regain the clarity to live the aligned, happy, healthy, and truly successful lives they're seeking and enjoy inner peace. Essentially, they consistently heal, grow, and thrive.

The more we can embrace these empowered masculine and feminine leadership traits, the more we AND our next generation can truly thrive and live Life Unlimited™.

Sally Dibden is the founder of The Wellbeing Consultants, a global Health Consulting, Life Coaching, Physiotherapy, and Pilates practice. She specialises in supporting dynamic achievers worldwide to optimise body and mind, so that they can enjoy consistent success and fulfilment, **with** great health and **without** burning out.

For over 20 years, Sally has worked in the fields of health, sport, and personal development, helping thousands of men and women return to top form and maintain it. She supports her patients and clients to deal with an array of issues exacerbated by stress such as anxiety, hormonal disturbances, persistent pain, emotional eating, communication problems, and under-performance. She helps them to set and achieve purposeful goals, connect with themselves, and learn the tools required to fully heal, grow, and thrive.

She lives between the French Alps and Lake Geneva, with her husband and children.

If you would you like to re-align and re-balance your body, mind, or life, then join her free, online '5 Step Energy

Kickstart': https://sallydibden.lpages.co/energy-kickstart-2018/

Otherwise connect with Sally at:

www.thewellbeingconsulants.com

www.facebook.com/TheWellbeingConsultant

www.instagram.com/sally_thewellbeingconsultant/

Just Keep Swimming
By Lori Granito

The first thing that went through my mind when they called my name was, "Lord, please don't let me trip when I walk up there!" We were seated at the back of the room, so I had to weave through quite a few tables to get to the front of the ballroom. I walked up the stairs (thankfully, without tripping) and stood on a stage in front of 500 people at the Four Seasons hotel in Hong Kong, the city I've called home for the last 26 years. I took a deep breath, looked out at the room, and marveled at just how I had gotten there.

I was on that stage to accept my second award for Entrepreneur of the Year – this one for the American Chamber's Women of Influence for my various restaurant ventures and for my work mentoring other women entrepreneurs through organizations like the Women Business Owners Club and the Women Entrepreneur's Network. I was getting ready to give my third TEDx talk the weekend after that awards ceremony. Little did I know, that less than six months later, I would go on to give a fourth talk. Life was good.

I had multiple thriving businesses in the restaurant industry, and previously was featured in publications like *Newsweek, Essence,* the *Asian Wall Street Journal*, and made appearances on CNN, CNBC, and Bloomberg television. I was also a contestant on *The Biggest Loser Asia*. As I accepted that award, I felt proud of myself, but also exhilarated and scared, all at the same time. I was proud because I remembered where I came from, all that I had gone through and overcome to get there. I remembered the people who lifted me up, and those who had tried to keep me down. I thought about the little girl I once was, growing up in the projects in New Orleans, in an area that was devastated by Hurricane Katrina. And I thought about that same little girl, who once overheard our neighbor telling my mother, who worked two or three jobs to put my siblings and me through private schools, that she was wasting her time spending so much money on books for me because I would probably wind up 16 and pregnant, like many of the other girls in the public-housing complex where we lived.

I was exhilarated and scared because I knew that I was preparing to leave most of the organizations that I received accolades and awards for, to begin a new venture. I was about to step WAY out of my comfort zone, and into the unknown with a new business, in a new industry. But it was a new business, that I knew in my bones and in my soul, was my true calling, and that would allow me to help and impact so many more women entrepreneurs through my new work as a professional speaker and a business and leadership coach.

You see as an entrepreneur, I was used to taking risks and had gone through a lot of ups and downs. Some of those falls cut so deeply I thought I'd never be able to get back up. After successfully opening and running my signature New Orleans style Cajun restaurant, The Bayou for several years, I decided to branch out with a second live-music restaurant venture. Right before opening that second venture in 2001, the Asian financial crisis hit, followed a few months later by September

11. Like many other businesses during that period, my companies' revenues were negatively affected.

So, by the end of 2001, I came to the painful realization that my businesses were failing. I was a new mom, but my first restaurant, The Bayou, was my other baby.

The first year we opened we made over US$1.6 million and had a good six-year run after that. I fed the likes of Roberta Flack, The Rolling Stones, James Brown, Vidal Sassoon, and Harry Connick Jr. I poured my heart and soul into that place for six years. It was where I celebrated the birth of my daughter and mourned the death of my brother. That restaurant was home. I was devastated the day that it closed. High rents, the SARS and bird flu outbreaks, plus the financial crisis eventually took its toll.

I remember calling my mom, crying about how we'd lost everything. Honestly, I was looking for sympathy and for her to share in my pity-party. I forgot who I was speaking to. My mother is a living, breathing testament to the power of resilience, and never lets anything, not even cancer, stand in her way. Anyone who knows my mother could tell you that between running multiple businesses, starting her own non-profit mentoring organization, and drag racing muscle cars on the weekend, she's a busy woman who does not have a lot of time for pity-parties. She said to me very matter-of-factly, "Lori, stop crying. I'm going to tell you two things: First, you know that every successful business owner that has ever made it big goes bust at some point. Just look at it this way – at least you got that over with! Now you just have to fall forward." Well, I didn't even have a chance to register the lesson she was trying to teach me, because the second thing she told me was, "Oh, and if you're planning on coming back home, you'd better make sure you have a job because you can't live here!"

So, I knew, one way or another, I had to make things work.

Despite that advice, I just plodded along for a few years, shrinking deeper into my self-imposed isolation and depression. Without even realizing it, I allowed my business failure to define and limit me. In many ways, it incapacitated me. We were SO broke, and the anxiety attacks that I sometimes had made it hard to breathe. I felt like I was constantly drowning, and I remember those times as very, very dark days.

I'm not proud to admit that at one point I even thought my husband and baby girl would be better off without me. Sometimes when it feels like you've been buried in a deep, dark place though, you don't even realize that you've actually been planted. The grass is always greener where you water it, and unfortunately, I had left my mental 'lawn' to wither.

The funny thing is that all the while this mental self-flagellation was going on, everyone around me thought I was supermom. My daughter was the first kid in her playgroup to be completely potty-trained, which made me a mommy rock-star. The other moms had no idea it was because I couldn't afford to buy diapers! In fact, my reality check came the day I went down to the ATM machine to get out $100 Hong Kong Dollars to buy diapers (about $12 USD), and I only had HK$97 in my account. So, I had to walk into the bank, line up, and write a check at the counter to withdraw the few remaining dollars in my account).

As I left the bank, I kept seeing the smirk on the teller's face as she slid the money across the counter to me. I walked back up the steep hill to get home, in the middle of the August heat, because I didn't even have the few coins needed to catch the bus. I beat myself up by playing that scene over and over in my head, so that by the time I reached my door, I was drenched not just in sweat, but in humiliation. I relieved the neighbor that was babysitting my daughter and decided that I needed a good cry and the last dregs of the cheap Paul Masson wine that was in my fridge.

My daughter was two-years old at the time, and as anyone with small kids knows, if you want some 'alone time' to go and drown your sorrows, all you have to do is put on your kid's favorite movie. Again, and again, and again. My daughter's favorite movie at the time was *Finding Nemo,* so I sat her in front of the TV, grabbed my wine, and sat on my bed. I was surrounded by bills -- final notices for electricity, water, gas, as well as credit card bills that would make your head spin. We were over US$250K in debt. How did it get to this point and how would we get out of it?

Always a multi-tasker, as I cried my eyes out, I also mentally calculated how many pots of water I'd need to boil on the portable gas camping burner to give my daughter a bath when the gas was cut off the next day. Somehow, through the nose-blowing and the tears, I heard this little voice singing along to the movie, "Just keep swimming, just keep swimming, just keep swimming, swimming..."

Now I probably should not be making it public, but I do have full-fledged conversations with myself. So, right then, I said to myself, "Lori, what the hell are you doing? You can't continue on like this. You've gotta get a grip, girl!"

It was at that moment that I decided to really try to move forward. I had come to the end of my rope, but still had to figure out a way to hang on. I would love to be able to tell you that my inspiration for moving forward again was something like finding a wonderful mentor, or winning the lottery, as opposed to an Ellen Degeneres voiceover of a memory-challenged fish.

But the truth is, I knew in that moment that I could get bitter, or I could get better. I knew that I had to make a choice, to either deal with what was thrown at me and let it make me stronger, or to continue hiding from the present circumstances and let it break me. My motivation was the realization that giving up would have been the real failure.

You don't really get to appreciate the bad things that happen in your life as part of the journey while they're happening. I'd forgotten that I had as many chances to take a leap of faith and try again as I chose to have. I let the bruising I'd taken with my failure scare me.

The truth is, that for all of us, every day is a clean slate. We have a chance to soar or a chance to fail and learn. Picking yourself back up is not easy. But what looks like failure may just be clearing a path to your life's work. Everything you're going through in that moment is preparing you for everything you're meant to be.

Coming through the challenge of failing and needing to start over from scratch is why I decided to help others as a mentor and coach. As a result of my work, women entrepreneurs learn to "Make their mess their message," and to grow and scale their businesses, so that they can impact the world.

I believe it's important for more women entrepreneurs to 'make their mess their message' because someone, somewhere, is going through the exact same thing as they may have gone through and needs to hear their story. For those women who are not at the point of being able to tell their story yet, because they're still in their mess, know that this too will pass. Focus on what you can do, with what you have, not on what you can't, with what you don't. It's scary sharing our screw-ups. We're afraid of what people will think and how they will judge us. Just know that everything you want lies on the other side of that fear. There comes a point where you just have to stop being so afraid of what could go wrong and start being positive about what could go right. Playing it safe is the enemy of greatness.

You see, despite all the things that it may have looked like I failed at, I'm an optimist at heart. Optimists see failures as learning experiences and challenges. They don't take failures personally or see them as evidence of some deep-seated character flaw. Being an optimist also allowed me to understand what my mother meant about falling forward; it's just picking yourself back up a few steps ahead of where you fell down. Life is too short to worry about the broken pieces of yesterday. When we refuse to give up, life presents us with an abundant sea of opportunity.

No matter where your journey takes you or how scary it is to start over, you have to remember how to dip your toes in the water and try new things out. Dive in and take long, broad strokes towards your dreams. You will hit rough waters –

that's a given. There may even be times when you feel like you're just treading water or drowning in a sea of overwhelming circumstances. Just remember that every storm passes, and even the choppiest waters eventually return to calm. So, if you're in those rough waters, or you're not sure which course you should take, just keep swimming and you'll eventually get to where you want to be.

Lori Granito is a four-time TEDx Speaker, a two-time Entrepreneur of the Year Award winner, professional speaker, and million-dollar business builder. She is the founder of Legendary Coaching and the Boss Lady Millionaires Club (http://www.bossladymillionairesclub.com/).

Her mission is to help increase the percentage of women running million-dollar businesses by sharing their message, scaling their businesses, and impacting the world. She does this by helping them spread their message on high-profile stages like TEDx, up-leveling their confidence and mindset, and creating customized, actionable business strategies to grow their businesses.

Lori is originally from New Orleans but has lived in Hong Kong for over 25 years. Her businesses have been featured in publications such as *Travel and Leisure, Time, Newsweek, Forbes, Essence,* and *The Robb Report*. Her television appearances include CNBC's *The Winners*, CNN's *Global Office* program, a six-week run on Bloomberg's *Asia Confidential*, and as a contestant on *The Biggest Loser Asia.*

Find her at www.lorigranito.com

Full Circle
By Angela Irwin

I was sitting at a table, on a screened-in porch in southwest Florida one evening in December, when my friend Kathy gently asked, "Are you okay?" We've been friends for close to 15 years, but since I had lived in France for the past six years and she in Florida, we didn't get to spend time in person very often. I had attended a professional event nearby and just spent the past couple of days with her. I immediately felt a bit alarmed at her question, and sticking with my go-to MO since childhood, I smiled and replied, "Of course, I'm fine! Why?" She answered, "You just don't seem like yourself." Internal alarms started to sound in my head. Crap, had I not been doing a good enough job at appearing "fine?" My instinct was to double-down and convince her all was well with me.

But, realizing I was in safe company with this dear friend, I let my guard down and admitted I was stressed and nervous about the complete career change I had undertaken at the beginning of the year. I underestimated the emotional implications that come up when you start your own business; doubly so when you go through training to become a life coach. Emotions I suppressed for decades hit me like a city bus.

I think I shared a few doubts like, "Would I actually be successful with this new career?" And "Should I have just stuck with what I knew and found another job in the medical devices field?" The conversation was all a blur. The next thing I remember is that she pulled out her iPhone and read a list of symptoms of depression. By this point, my reflexes, having been so vulnerable, were at Defcon One, and I just wanted to shut the conversation down. Shaking my head, I thought, "No. NO! I'm not depressed! That's crazy!" Until it wasn't. I sat there in stunned silence as she continued through the list. And then the tears came. My mind tried to reconcile the absolute disbelief that *I* could be experiencing depression versus the sudden clarity of the all-too-familiar symptoms she just read.

I made one last-ditch effort to refute her observation. "I can't be depressed; the name of my business is Joyful Life Solutions!" But even as I said the words, I knew she was right. The months of my uncharacteristic behavior finally made sense: not leaving the house or even showering, sometimes for days at a time; the erratic sleeping patterns; the disregard for everyday things, like eating regularly, doing laundry, and cleaning the house; my inability to do things for my business that I knew were critical. It's frightening to find yourself in a state where you can't even recognize the person behaving the way that you are. And even more frightening, is when you are unable to *will* yourself to take action. It's as if I was wearing cement clothes for all the success I had in getting myself to make the next move.

As my friend's words sank it, I felt momentary relief that this behavior I was experiencing had a name. For the past six months, I just thought I suddenly had become the laziest person on the planet. And I loathed that person. Looking back, that loathing actually fueled the depression.

Unbeknownst to me, changing my career and starting my own business brought up a tidal wave of unaddressed emotions stemming back decades. Let me explain.

*****

I was born with normal hearing and learned to speak normally. But in first grade, the annual hearing exam revealed that I had a mild hearing loss. My parents were stunned but reassured that the hearing loss would not progress. That prediction did not end up being true. Over the course of the next 15 years, I *slowly* went deaf.

During that time, my speech began to change. By 6th grade, I was made fun of for the way my speech sounded, and upon meeting new people, I was regularly asked, "Why do you talk funny?" This made me burn with embarrassment and shame. I silently berated myself and wondered why I couldn't just be like everyone else. This feedback taught me to be seen and not heard, that it wasn't safe to speak up or be visible, because being shamed was the result.

Hearing loss in children usually happens in one of two ways: 1) they are born with it/genetics, or 2) an illness or injury causes it. I had neither of those reasons, and to this day, the cause of my hearing loss is unexplained. My parents took me to every audiologist and ENT in our four-state area to try to get answers. Every one of them said the same two things: "We've never seen this before in a child, and we don't know why she continues to lose more hearing." As a child, hearing those statements over and over and over, I interpreted them to mean I was flawed, that I was fundamentally broken. **These**

beliefs were the foundation of my low self-worth, self-esteem, and self-confidence.

My parents were told that I wouldn't graduate from high school, and some years later they also were told not to encourage me to go to college because I would just flunk out. More than one person advised my parents they needed to force me to "accept my fate" and learn sign language, as that would be my only option for communication in the future.

However, despite these predictions, I graduated from mainstream high school with "high honors," graduated from college in four years, and was on the Dean's list all four years. I was also a cheerleader for football and men's basketball, and had a full-time job in college. I went on to earn my Master's Degree while working full-time. I don't share this information to be boastful, but rather to give hope that it's possible to beat a prognosis given by professionals. I was determined to prove them all wrong.

It seems strange looking back, but over the course of those 15 years, the fact that I was losing my hearing was never discussed with me. Once a year, I had a hearing test to monitor the extent of my loss, but for the other 364 days per year, it was not talked about. From my perspective, this lack of communication was a coping mechanism. If I didn't acknowledge that I was going deaf, then it wasn't really happening. As a child, I didn't have the tools to deal with the emotions, and no one talked to me about hearing loss, so I felt like it was my solo burden. I carried the fear and shame alone, acting like everything was fine, while inside I was absolutely terrified about what would happen to me. I blamed myself for what was taking place. I believed that I was somehow causing my hearing to deteriorate.

Most of the time, I just pushed forward with blind faith that somehow, some way, I would be able to remain in the "hearing world." There were times when I felt like, "What's the point of bothering to study for this test?" The writing was on the wall that I was going deaf. What was the point of preparing for the future when I didn't feel like I would have one? My biggest fear during those years was that my only future would be living in my parent's basement on their farm near a town of 1200 people. While it was a great place to grow up, I'd had dreams of living in a big city and traveling the world since elementary school. But if I couldn't hear, I would be cut off from the world. What kind of job could I have if I couldn't hear, communicate, or use the phone? And with no job, what kind of future could I possibly have?

Then, at the age of 23, a miracle happened. I received a cochlear implant—first in one ear followed by one in the other ear several years later. This technology essentially gave me a second chance at life. After 15 years of losing my hearing, I suddenly regained it. It's hard to articulate how surreal that process was. It was as if my world had gone from black and white to technicolor. I heard sounds I hadn't heard in years and sounds I had never heard, due to developments in technology. For example, I could once again hear the sound that soda makes—that fizzing when you pour it over ice. And I realized that the copy machine in the office beeped when it was out of paper! Regaining the ability to use the phone was absolutely priceless. This was before texting and email, so the phone was the only way to communicate at the time. I got my independence back and no longer had to rely on others to make phone calls for me. I'm beyond grateful to live during the time when cochlear implant technology is possible. Without my cochlear implants, my career opportunities and life experiences would have been much more limited.

*****

Returning home to France from Florida, I thought that since I knew I was experiencing depression, I would just be able to get over it. Unfortunately, emotions don't work that way. The depression actually got worse before it got better because I thought I could just handle it on my own. The idea that I was depressed was simply another thing I beat myself up about.

I finally talked to a therapist who explained that the body remembers emotional trauma and reacts accordingly. By starting a new career that spotlighted me, I unintentionally managed to replicate the exact feelings that were present during my 15 years of losing my hearing: fear, isolation, uncertainty about the future, along with low self-worth and self-confidence. The memories of being shamed when I spoke as I was losing my hearing came roaring back, and subconsciously I was convinced the same thing would happen if I was visible. It felt as if I was no longer a grown woman, but rather that terrified little girl who was trying to run the show.

One of the most frustrating aspects for me was realizing that emotions are not logical. As someone who operated the majority of my life in a masculine mode, the idea that I couldn't simply *will* these negative feelings to subside was incredibly frustrating.

In my 15-year corporate career in the medical devices industry, I had a decent amount of success. I received many promotions and won numerous internal awards. I was able to "mask" my confidence well enough. And I was pretty bold in life. I loved skydiving, traveled the world, and even accepted a job transfer in France, despite not knowing a soul there or speaking the language. I thought to myself, "You have done all of those things, surely you can do something as simple as tell people about your new career!" But, my emotions were not logical, and it seemed as if all those successes and experiences I'd had were done by a different person.

In order to alleviate the depression, I had to work through those 15 years of suppressed emotions and feelings. These negative feelings were exacerbated by the need in my new career to be very visible on social media as part of my marketing. Throughout my corporate career I did a significant amount of public speaking, and really enjoyed it. But it's entirely different being visible and speaking about the great products of the companies I worked for vs. essentially presenting me and my services as the product.

So, I addressed the emotions and negative beliefs about myself head-on with some amazing professional support. This process was extremely painful at times because making these changes took a diligent effort to reprogram my decades-old beliefs and feelings.

As I worked on myself, it suddenly seemed like nearly every woman I spoke with talked about experiencing issues with her own confidence. By all outer appearances, these were amazing, successful women, from all over the world, who admitted to feeling insecure. I remember thinking, "This problem is like an epidemic, but no one is talking about it." I decided to pivot my life coaching to primarily focus on helping women to build their core confidence muscle. Yes, it is a muscle that can be built, but I didn't know that until I went through rebuilding my own confidence. Ironically, I thought I'd be the last person on earth to help others improve their confidence, but because I have gone through the process myself, I now embrace that I'm the perfect person to do so.

I am determined to turn up the global conversation about women and confidence. Finding our inner strength is such an important skill. How we feel about ourselves impacts every aspect of our lives—our relationships, our decision making, our work performance, lifestyle choices, and mood. By improving the way we view ourselves, and by building our self-confidence, everything else can improve, as well. I don't want even ONE person to experience the negative view that I previously felt about myself at times.

I've truly come full circle. I love the quote from Tony Robbins, "Things don't happen to you, they happen *for* you." Through the most difficult aspects of my life and most painful emotional experiences, I can help others. At the end of the day, I believe that everything I've been through led me to this place: equipped to help others step into their best, boldest, most confident selves. To see people blossom, step up their confidence, and be bolder in their lives is an amazing experience to be a part of.

Angela Irwin is an international Life Coach, TEDx speaker, and the founder of Joyful Life Solutions, which specializes in helping women who are looking for support to achieve their goals and gain more clarity, confidence, and fulfillment in life.

Prior to that, Angela spent 15 years in the corporate medical device field, holding various positions in marketing, management, and clinical education in the United States, Australia, and Europe.

Angela is particularly passionate about helping people unleash their self-confidence, achieve their goals, and be bolder in life. She supplements her training by drawing from her personal experiences, numerous challenges, and transitions in her own life.

In addition to her coaching training, Angela holds B.S. degrees in sociology and psychology, as well as an M.B.A.

Born in a small farming community in South Dakota, Angela has lived and traveled all over the world. She and her husband Colin have lived in France for the past eight years.

You can connect with Angela here:

https://www.facebook.com/joyfullifesolutions/

www.joyfullifesolutions.com

Subscribe to her podcast, the *Authentic Connection Chronicles: Stories of Courage, Vulnerability & Failure* here:

https://joyfullifesolutions.clickfunnels.com/landing_podcast_jls20162023

Be a Success Story
By Dijana Jovanoska

"The leadership position must not be given to her, in any way! I'll make her lose!" the man called out in a full voice. He wanted that job, a special leadership position in the company, more than anything. Others around him disagreed by saying that she met all the conditions for the job. They asked him not to make a scene in the café. It would be better for him to calm down and accept reality.

"No!" He called out angrily, paying no attention to other people who were guests in the café. He did not even know that I was present there with my friends. He did not know because he was too upset to recognize us.

He didn't care that he offended us. He didn't even know that we were sitting with the woman who received the leadership position that he wanted. He did not even know our character or that we too were professionals. Of course, we did not matter to him; he only focused on his belief that SHE should not have the leadership position. He wanted it for himself.

Did he honestly believe that a man would be more successful in that position than a woman?

Even though he never met the new leader, he thought that he could gain her position through threats and turmoil.

Did he feel threatened because he used political means to gain his position, and he did not accomplish it himself through his own hard work? He obviously believed that his newly acquired power gave him the right to grab what he didn't deserve or could achieve through his own ability.

Would he use his new power to show strength, with the intent to intimidate?

"Yes, it certainly seems that way," I thought as we left the café.

Aware of the drama he was causing, we slipped out, unnoticed.

My friend, who had just received her new position, was very surprised at the dramatic scene we witnessed and wanted to give up her job from the start.

But I didn't allow it. I supported her fully, especially since I knew what kind of man he was. "We can make your job a success together," I told her. "You should not give up."

From that evening on, I knew that we would have to deal with that bully and manipulator, who would fight in every way to take that job away from her. For bullies, it is easy to fight against someone they don't even know, because that person doesn't matter to them. Bullies use every tool they have against their imagined "enemy," including lies and manipulation.

I knew my friend would soon be attacked by that man's manipulative skills and fictitious lies. How could she deal with him when she didn't know how to combat his lies or manipulation? Thankfully, I knew how to help her.

"I will fight to keep my position," she said. "I won't give up. But, I need your help; I'll follow your guidance step-by-step. I want you to advise me on how to outwit him."

"Then, we will always be one step ahead," I replied.

My friend hired me to help coach her as a client. I knew how to help her handle this manipulator, who she had to deal with professionally, because I had dealt with manipulators before.

She was a successful leader, and he was a new politician in our hometown. Although her work was closely related to his, I did not want him to have any impact on her professional managerial decisions. I didn't want the bully to have a chance to influence her leadership position, because he would not contribute anything positive to her work. If she accepted favors from him, it could be the end of the success and authority that she acquired through years of hard work. Because of his manipulative skills she needed to keep her mind clear and use her power to resist him when necessary.

It was easy for her to control her emotions, because she previously studied my program, "Learn How to Perceive People." She followed all the steps that she learned in the course and applied them to her profession to achieve success.

We decided to keep him away from her professional life and not allow him any influence in the company she managed. His influence, however, was unavoidable because he was a politician, and in my country the politicians have influence everywhere they want. But, she was firmly resolved in her decision.

"It's better to avoid contact with him, even if it might hurt your position," I said. We were aware that his influence as a politician could ruin her reputation, and his manipulations could hurt her business.

She accepted my advice immediately because that was how she dealt with life. She was determined to be independent, to retain her freedom. As you know, a successful leader never obeys advice that has no value. A successful leader does not follow someone who does not share their values, someone who wants to gain their position through lies and manipulation.

I worked closely with her to create a wonderful program that would improve her situation personally and professionally.

I believed in her ability to succeed, even though she was a little afraid of his influence and power as politician.

My friend started working at a level that the bully could not comprehend. He was only interested in the power that somebody else could provide for him, like in the political party he belonged to. But he didn't understand that there might be a different kind of power that my client acquired personally through years of hard work, knowledge gained through experience, and values that no one could disturb or reduce. He was not aware that this kind of power was greater and more real than the power he gained through political favors. But he was blind to this discrepancy, because his sole focus was to destroy her and remove her from her job.

She was nervous waiting for the day when they would meet. She wondered how he would treat her. She wondered which direction he would lead the conversation. He did not know my friend at all, but he already was her greatest enemy.

Their first meeting went just as I expected. The same man, who made such a scene in the café, acted politely and cordially, promising to give her support in everything that she did. He offered her unconditional help in every area, and said she was the right choice for that position.

But I knew his manner was just for show. I was sure that she was dealing with a manipulator and all the problems that relationship presented. Since my program is designed to deal with manipulators, it was a perfect fit for her situation. She was determined that he would not influence the decisions she made for her company. She realized that working through her professional hurdles would help her become more successful than ever.

There followed a period of four years in which his manipulations continued until they reached their peak. Just when she thought that her manipulator had reached his goal, he introduced even greater lies and manipulations directed towards her.

When you live in a small town, it is easy to spread rumors and lies to make people appear in the wrong light. But ruining her reputation wasn't as easy as he imagined. For years, my friend had built authority and influence in her company and within the circle of people she knew well. It was not easy for a newly emerging influence, namely the bully, to break her already-established image. She didn't worry about those who didn't know her personally because they had no place in her professional or private life.

She kept her distance from him so he could not to affect her psyche or success. How did his lies affect her? She ignored them all, leaving her success to speak for itself. She heard from others about the rumors he tried to spread about her work and credibility. But he never slandered her in person. He was always very correct and polite at their meetings.

The bully's lies were always shallow and easy to see through, so my client was able to ignore them. He once spread a rumor that she would not be able to pay her employees one month, due to a high turnover in employment. She spent a short period of time reassuring her employees that they should not be afraid. She would always provide salaries while she was in leadership. Each month they continued to receive a salary, so that after the second month, the employees realized that these rumors were just his fictitious lies.

She also had to refute his lie that she used her position and power to help her son get a job within the company. Initially, this lie again brought the resentment of the employees and others in our small town because they thought it was unfair that she might abuse her influence this way. But soon, everyone realized the truth, and the lie could not remain alive. Her son did not live in our city, nor even in our country. He worked abroad and had lived there for almost a year.

The bully also lied that she did not attend meetings during a moment of crisis when floods hit our town because she wasn't responsible and didn't care about the people living there. Only those without a clue bought into this stupid rumor. During that period, she was abroad for a family celebration, and she led her team from there through phone calls and emails. Every meeting concerning the flood was attended by a man from her team so she could stay aware of the situation.

These were lies that she could simply ignore, because time alone proved that they were simply fiction, fabricated by a manipulator. If lies undermine your authority or success, then you must react, but if they are superficial and easily visible, they will not carry far, and your deeds and integrity will speak for themselves.

But with these lies and many other fabricated stories, he tried to manipulate others to destroy her authority. He wanted to get her out of that position before she could be elected by the Minister of Health.

But he did not bring her down. He only managed to reveal his manipulative character, nothing else. He failed to damage her reputation or affect her psyche. He failed to draw her into his manipulative world and destroy her. He failed to tarnish her accomplishments as a leader or the success of the company she led. She didn't let him destroy her life. She continued to manage the company effectively while her work became even more successful.

***

I share this story with you to explain that you can accomplish everything you want. But to truly succeed you must know how to recognize people from the beginning, how to manage your emotions and values, how to keep your inner power, and how to keep manipulators and toxic people a safe distance from you. By following this advice, you will know how to be successful with others, and you will always be a step ahead of manipulators and toxic people.

I do not respect people with newly-gained power who hide their ignorance behind manipulations, lies, and demonstrations of strength. I do not respect a man who uses his influence, that someone else gave to him, even the most powerful politician in my country, by trying to manipulate a woman. But, there are strong women that such manipulators encounter that will not be overwhelmed; not everyone can be subdued.

A woman who creates her own power, who is independent and does not have to rely on anyone, is a woman who cannot be broken. She is always a step ahead of manipulation and intimidation.

A woman in leadership is often the target of manipulators. Because of the motivation for sexual or political power, or the desire for influence and leadership, the manipulator must first ruin her personality and weaken her success. It is therefore very important to recognize the character of people around you from the first impression, to determine what kind of people they have contact with. What kind of people do you allow into your professional and private life? Be very careful. Choose your colleagues and friends preventively. Always keep in touch with the people who share your same values. Do not make a place for negative people in your life.

When you know how to recognize a person's character in the first moment, then you will be able to make better decisions. As a leader you will be able to choose the best team for your company or group. As a woman, your private life will always be filled with people who love you and understand you.

Never reduce your principles and standards to seem more appealing to others who not share your values. You should not lower your standards, even for those who are your superiors or have political power. Each time you lower the standards or values, you only make room for toxic people in your life. You do not need them.

Be who *you* are. Be powerful in your own values and skills. You are the leader of your life. Only you can manage your life and your emotions. Do not give the steering wheel of your life to anyone else. Keep total control over your career and your private life.

Is a powerful career only for men? No. Both men and women can have a successful career, inspiring employees and bringing innovative ideas for the future success of the company.

Do you believe that a woman can't have a successful professional life as well as a fulfilling private life? No, that's not the truth. Both are absolutely possible, but she must have the winning skill: the ability to perceive people. With this tool, she will always be successful at work with her team and happy at home with her family and friends. She will not feel stress and will have enough free time to relax and unwind. She will be fulfilled. She will know how to recognize manipulators and never have a place in her life for them. The winning skill is priceless. It's her treasure.

In order to achieve the winning skill for yourself, be sure to follow these steps:

- Never leave problems unresolved nor give them more emphasis than they should have. Remember, for every problem there is a solution if you keep a positive attitude, stay calm, and position good people around you.
- Refuse to allow toxic people or manipulators to enter your life from the start. You should never again allow manipulative and toxic people to ruin you as a person or to ruin your psyche. You can be free from this burden if you recognize them from their first

impression. Say, "NO!" to those manipulative people who try to enter your life, uninvited. Create a completely new world in which you live without toxic people.

- Save your energy. Do not let your energy be spent on unimportant situations or people. NOW is the time to take your life into your own hands. Do not leave this important decision until tomorrow; do not wait another moment. You alone are the creator of your life.
- Love yourself. Love yourself for all your strengths and weaknesses. Improve your strengths each day, and step-by-step, overcome your weaknesses. Never highlight your flaws in front of people you first meet. Wait until you know if these people are manipulators who will use your weaknesses against you. If you open the door of your life to the right people, you will be able to overcome your short-comings together. If you do not recognize someone as a manipulator and bring him into your life, he might ruin you.

It is my desire for you to have a successful professional and private life. You have come into this world for this purpose. You are someone who knows how to manage your own life.

That's why my most important advice to you is to learn how to perceive people. When you know how to understand them at the very beginning, then you will find true success. Knowing how to determine the character of people will determine whether you will have a peaceful life or a life full of stress.

Always surround yourself with the best team in your workplace and the best people in your private life.

Never stop learning. Be a successful woman in all areas of your life.

Only you can help yourself. The sooner you understand this, the freer you will be to make all the right decisions.

Always be a success story.

Dijana Jovanoska is a business consultant, personal coach, author, and entrepreneur. She has a PhD in Economics. For many years, she has been a successful leader in Construction and Operations with residential and working spaces. She also was a manager in the Public Health Institution. With her online training program, Dijana helps others become successful leaders, constantly flourishing in their businesses, with exceptional private lives. She helps them to know the secret for success and a fulfilling life.

Her background includes over 20 years of leadership positions, business consulting, personal transformational coaching, financial and career problem-solving, various conferences and projects in her profession, and professional publications in finance and public health.

She lives in Macedonia with her husband and two sons.

Visit Dijana's website: www.thewinningskill.com

And join her Facebook Page:
www.facebook.com/thewinningskill

Book a free session call: www.thewinningskill.com/call

For all your questions contact her:
dijana@thewinningskill.com

The Basketball Game
By Lisa Nielsen

Never Give Up, Never Surrender. ~ Galaxy Quest

Being 14-years old was difficult. Not only was it difficult, but there were expectations I didn't understand. I realize now, I was expected to act grown-up, but I didn't know what being grown-up meant. Being half grown-up and half little child, I wasn't sure where I fit all the time. It's the same when you're an adult. It feels like we still should be children, and there are so many things about life and business that are unknowns.

At fourteen, I was a chubby-ish, short child with long brown hair and hazel eyes. I felt like I was a normal child with nothing that stood out about me. I was average. There was a place in the kitchen where my family left messages for each other. The phone hung on the wall and had a very long cord that could be stretched out. If anyone wanted privacy, we would take the handset and pull it as far into the laundry room as possible. Stretching the cord this way, gave me the ability to talk on the phone without many people overhearing my conversation. Because of the positioning of the phone, there weren't many secrets between my siblings and myself. So, it wasn't a secret that I loved to watch most athletic events, but rarely liked to participate.

One day, there was a message for me, written by my Dad. It said "Basketball Game tomorrow at 2. I'll take you." My heart sank. I loved watching basketball, I understood the rules, I felt it was a very good game to play if you liked to be active and healthy. However, basketball wasn't something I liked to play. There was a basketball hoop on the side of our driveway where my older two brothers played basketball. From time to time, they got me to play too. They dribbled the ball around me, and I got very frustrated trying to keep up and make a basket. They beat me every time I played against them.

Knowing that I wasn't great at basketball made me dread my upcoming game. I decided to see if I could get out of playing, but after making a few phone calls, I realized the team needed me to show up. Without me, there wouldn't be enough players, and the team would have to forfeit the game. In my heart, I felt I would make them lose anyway, but decided the team needed to have the chance to at least compete.

How many times in business do you feel this way? Do you feel sometimes like you don't want to show up to work that day? But after trying not to work, you get sucked into working anyway? Those days are worth the effort to show up and do your best. You need the chance to compete, to do your best, and have the results you desire.

The next afternoon, I arrived with my Dad and my youngest brother at the church where we played basketball. We were a little early, and I felt the nervousness creeping into my stomach. The coach was excited to see me. I loved the social aspect of participating in the game. I made friends playing this sport. I liked my team, I liked my coach, I liked a lot of things about basketball. As I looked around at my team mates and counted them, I realized there were barely enough of us to make a team. We would all have to play the whole game without any substitutes. It was going to be a grueling game. Logic told me the other team was better than we were. I knew they practiced more than we did. They had won more games. But, our coach told us we were as good as they were. She had been the coach for over a year, and she knew our abilities, and our weaknesses. She knew where we were strong, and I counted on her wisdom. We believed her when she said we were as good as our opponents, even though logic said otherwise.

When I have a manager, who knows my strengths and weaknesses, I believe that manager. I trust the judgement of that manager more than others who don't know me as well. If you are a manager, be sure to have a real appreciation for your people. Know their strengths and help them to understand what they do well. If you have a manager who may not understand your assets, be sure to help them see where you are strong. You have strengths, even if you would rather not play the game they are playing.

It was time for the tipoff, and we got the ball. I was relieved to see my teammates were a lot better at dribbling than I was, and they were happy to take off in the correct direction. At times, I lost track of which basket was ours, and it felt that I was just running in circles. Several times I shot the ball at the wrong basket, but luckily didn't score. The ball was stolen from us, but we stole it back. The ball changed hands; we fouled our opponents, and they fouled us. The turnovers, steals, and fouls seemed to be one for one. Yet, I was afraid that my lack of skill might cost the game. We were evenly matched, but I doubted my ability and wasn't sure I could physically last until halftime.

My lack of skill for dribbling was my biggest fear. I was afraid my opponents would be able to take the ball too many times and score a lot of points. But that didn't happen. My fear of dribbling was something I shouldn't have been so worried about. Every time I had the chance to look at the score, it was tied. TIED! It was a close game. During one of the time-outs, the coach mentioned to be careful to not foul out. If we did, we wouldn't have enough girls to play, and we would lose. She told us teamwork is important when you feel you might lose. She reminded us to work together and remember each other's strengths. There were so many ways to lose in this game.

In business, do you ever feel you can't win? That the cards are stacked against you? Do you worry about things that might never happen? Sometimes I feel that my presentation is off, or that I really didn't make the point I was hoping to make. Sometimes I walk out of a meeting for a new account I hope to land, and I'm positive I didn't get the account. Later, in my car, I say to myself, "Here's where you can improve next time." Sometimes it's such a terrible presentation, I wish I had asked someone else to do it for me. But if others do it for me, then I don't learn. Part of the success is failing. You have to fail a lot before you can be good at what you do.

There's a saying, "Fail Fast, Fail Often." If I can do something enough that I'm failing, that means that sometimes I succeed. I only need to succeed a few times to be able to do it right. More than once, I knew my presentation to an employer was lacking in detail or in content. Sometimes, I wouldn't address the issues they had. I left, thinking I didn't get the account. Most of the time, I was right, but I learned to ask better questions about the issues they might have. I addressed their questions about the details or content better after I failed a few times. It might feel terrible when you fail, but don't stop. Refusing to participate will let your team and those cheering you on down.

My Dad was my best cheerleader. I knew he loved and cared about me. I didn't want a casual friend or my siblings or even my Mom to be my cheerleader. I valued all their opinions; I knew they liked me or even loved me, but when it came to important things, I wanted my Dad to be there. I could always hear his voice. Even at a soft level, I could hear what he said from the sidelines. "Go right." "Pass the ball." "Shoot!" Mostly he yelled his encouragement at the top of his voice, but sometimes, at the most important moment`s, it was the quiet whisper, "You can do it." Those four words have stuck with me my entire lifetime, because I knew he wanted the best for me. Through the course of the game, my Dad cheered me on less and less. I thought his silence was because he lost his voice. Now I realize, I no longer needed the cheering. I was doing just fine on my own.

Choose the people who mentor you carefully. You want to be able to trust them and know they mean the best for you. In business, the best mentors sometimes aren't people who love you or care about you. But, they want to see you succeed; they will help you be your best self. Yet, there will come a time when they will feel their part is done and will let you go. Just know you can make it on your own. You can remember the lessons that were taught to you and follow the positive words that they imparted.

At halftime, the basketball game was still tied. The coach took the team aside to give us a pep talk. She said we were doing much better than she had hoped, and we could actually win the game. She let us know how much she appreciated all the extra effort on the court. We all agreed we had given our all. We ran, dribbled, shot the ball, were fouled, and fouled others. Every one of us. We were out of breath, out of energy, and out of hope.

But our coach let us know the plan for the next half. We needed to continue to play our best, while improving at passing and steals. The instructions were specific, timely, and achievable. We had renewed hope that we could win. The entire team sat on the bench, drinking water, when my Dad started passing around some granola mix he'd brought with him. It seemed to be the most heavenly snack I'd ever had in my life. It wasn't the ingredients, or the taste. It just happened to be what we all needed. A boost. We ate the entire bag of granola, then it was time to play again.

When you are working at your business or your job, do you ever feel you just need a boost? Something to recharge your work? When this happens to me, just changing a few things can help. Sometimes you just need a plan that has specific, timely, and achievable goals. Maybe one phrase in your report or presentation turns people away. It's worthwhile to video your presentation, take it to your office, and review what you've done. I tape myself often to see what I can improve. During my first video I saw I paced a lot more than I should. I also said "um" too many times. I even caught myself scratching my nose. Small changes at just the right time can make a huge difference. It pays to always review your material and update it to add a boost to your business.

The basketball game went on for what seemed forever. Still, whenever I looked at the score, we were always tied. We were doing our best. We kept up with the other team and at times we even out-played them. We needed to simply outlast them. To keep going when we wanted to give up. We weren't pretty at that moment. But honestly, I thought we actually weren't too bad looking. We were ragged, sure. We needed to rest, yes. But we were happy. We loved the teamwork, and the game was coming together for us. Some of us couldn't dribble to save our lives, but were a pretty good shot. Some were great at dribbling but not shooting. Some were great at knowing which basket was ours, and some of us knew more rules than others. Helping each other, we came together as a team. We each had our strengths and weaknesses. Surprisingly, I could actually shoot the ball. Not as well as some, but better than I thought. My teammates kept tossing the ball to me, and I'd shoot. I had one main purpose in the game: to stand under the correct basket and shoot the ball.

Find your one purpose that you are great at. If your gift is finding new clients, do that. If you excel at organizing data or encouraging others to do their best, do that. When your business is starting up, you probably need to know about everything. But then, you can fine-tune your skills and see what you're good at. You might need to hire someone who is great at doing the tasks that aren't your strengths, and that's okay, as long as you work together.

Suddenly, the ball got knocked out of bounds, and we had a brief moment to make a plan with the coach. She pointed out that we were still tied, and we only had a few seconds left in the game with no time-outs. She made a plan to get the ball to me before time ran out. As long as I didn't have to dribble, she was confident I would make a basket. I was a nervous wreck. The fate of the game was dependent on if I could make the basket at the last second of the game. It was a lot of pressure for a 14-year old girl who didn't like playing basketball in the first place.

As the ball was passed onto the court, the clock started. I took my place under the correct basket, waiting for the pass. My stomach was in knots, but I knew I needed to pull off the win for my team, my coach, and my Dad. The ball was passed to the dribbler. But the other team put so much pressure on her, she almost lost the ball. She recovered nicely, and I knew it was time to win the game. She passed the ball to me; I dribbled twice and shot the ball. The buzzer went off. The gym was silent as we all watched the ball go through the net. We cheered and screamed and laughed at the win. The other team congratulated us. Both teams enjoyed the game and were pleased with their efforts. I made some great friends from both teams that have lasted my entire lifetime.

The final score of the game? 2-0.

Do your best in business and in life. Sometimes the results are surprising.

Lisa B. Nielsen was born and raised in Salt Lake City, Utah. She attended Southern Utah State College where she met and married her sweetheart, Jim Nielsen. They spent 13 years raising three beautiful children together. In 1991, Jim had a massive stroke which he courageously survived. This stroke provided an opportunity to grow further than Lisa thought possible. For the next 25 years, Lisa was Jim's caregiver. Learning, compassion, patience, and business skills were her focus.

During the years when her children were small, Lisa spent many years working for a clinical laboratory, then eventually migrated into an Insurance supplement career, which she loves. In addition to her insurance business, Lisa is an advocate for disabled adults.

Lisa loves to travel, and is within reach of her life-long goal of visiting every state in the United States of America. She also loves to sing, and has performed with a community choir for most of the last 18 years.

Lisa is the mother of three adult children, and the grandmother of 11 grandchildren. She loves family life, and strives to stay close to them.

She is thankful for the unwanted trials, where she feels she has learned the biggest lessons in her life. These lessons bring her closer to the Lord, her family, and her core beliefs.

She can be contacted at lisanielsen01@gmail.com

The Most Important Skill & Secret to Success

By Jane Richardson, PhD

Do you feel misunderstood?
Are you judged by the things you say or don't say?

Do you feel like something is holding you back?
Are you afraid to use your voice and speak up for yourself?

Do you feel stuck with no relief in sight?
Are you frustrated by not reaching your fullest potential?

If you answered "yes" to any of these questions, we are alike. I spent decades feeling the same way.

I know exactly how it feels to be misunderstood; it's a horrible feeling.
I also have felt the judgment from things I said and even the things I didn't.

I know how limiting it feels to be held back.
I felt afraid to use my voice and speak up for myself, so I remained quiet.

I know how it feels not to have any relief in sight and see no light at the end of the tunnel.
I too felt limited because I wasn't reaching my fullest potential.

These feeling weren't always apparent to me. But over time, I realized I did not want to feel this way anymore. These harsh feelings began to have an impact on myself, my personality, and those around me. Unfortunately, I know these feelings all too well, as I have been there before, and I too have struggled through rough times. However, to get to where I am today, I had to recognize what I was feeling, realize why I felt that way, and determine how I could improve. Through self-reflection and courage, I realized I needed to change my perspective to change how I felt in life.

To apply this realization and make a change, I had to identify what the source of these feelings were. Throughout my childhood, I felt eclipsed. As the youngest of four children and the only girl, my stories about ice skating and sewing could never compare to the spirited and powerful tales the boys told at the dinner table. Over time, after years of being eclipsed as the family sat together each night, I lost my voice. I lost my will and courage to speak up, to talk about my day, or to explain how I felt. I lost the capacity and ability to communicate my thoughts, hopes, and dreams. By not communicating these aspects of my mind, I subjected myself to being misunderstood, judged, and overlooked.

Through a self-reflection period, I recognized I was not living up to my fullest potential. I spent many days suppressing myself and my voice. My feelings of being misunderstood, judged, and overlooked stemmed directly from my action of playing small. By playing small, I feared rejection daily. I knew my stories couldn't compare to those of the boys, so I did not have enough confidence to speak up due to fear of being put down and rejected. I did not want to have my stories interrupted or eclipsed, so I kept them to myself and refrained from opening up. I did not allow myself to speak up and feel empowered. As a result, I spent years playing small and did not do anything to change how I felt.

As I started to have the will and desire for change, I turned to a few role models for inspiration. On my hardest, most silent days, I channeled confidence and courage through the wise words of those I looked up to. Their inspiring words are below:

"Your playing small does not serve the world. There is nothing enlightened about shrinking so that other people won't feel insecure around you. We are all meant to shine."
~ Marianne Williamson

"The world doesn't need more people playing small. It's time to stop hiding out and start stepping out. It's time to stop needing and start leading. It's time to start sharing your gifts instead of hoarding them or pretending they don't exist. It's time you started playing the game of life in a 'big' way."
~ T. Harv Eker

"Give yourself permission to live a big life. Step into who you are meant to be. Stop playing small. You're meant for greater things."
~ Joan Burge

These words pushed me out of my comfort zone. They provided me with relief, confidence, and a desire for change. The various communication styles of those I looked up to spoke to me and helped me realize I needed to speak up for myself.

After I identified the cause and source of my feelings, I decided it was time to exercise what little courage I had left. I had to stop playing small. I was done feeling misunderstood, judged, and overlooked. It was my time to reach my fullest potential and speak up for myself. I decided it was time to clearly communicate.

How I Recognized My Fullest Potential
Playing small is a big problem. I spent decades in the vicious cycle of putting myself down, minimizing my importance, and not utilizing my voice. A serious change was required to stop playing small. Not only did that include a change emotionally, but also mentally.

I had to be brave and speak my mind. By doing so, I learned the power of communication. Being able to communicate my feelings, thoughts, and ideas was half the battle. To win this battle, I decided to utilize the voice I was given.

I gave gratitude for what I had been through. I allowed myself to heal and stand strong. I worked to gradually rebuild a foundation of value and worth within myself.

I embraced the process. I was patient with myself, and I allowed time to adapt to who I was meant to be. A new direction and lifestyle was ahead of me.

Most importantly, through a self-reflection period, I was able to implement and master the power of communication.

Communication is a form of art, a blessing from above, and a unique and essential skill. I hope the power of communication provides you with the same amount of courage and confidence as it did for me.

As you embark on your new adventure, change directions, and create a new lifestyle, I would like you to remember the following:

> You are, and always will be, your greatest creation.
> Why not aspire to create a well-spoken person?

Communication is Crucial
To rebuild myself and achieve my fullest potential, I needed to start improving my communication. You may ask, why is communication so crucial? It's crucial because learning how to communicate is the most important skill and the secret to success.

Communication opens the door to an unlimited amount of connections and understanding in your personal relationships and professional life.

As you become a well-spoken person who embarks on this new adventure, I would like you to begin implementing this skill. I realized communication was the most important skill when I read these four words by Dr. Paul Watzlawick, who eloquently demonstrated the significance of communication, stating,

> "One cannot not communicate."

In other words, even when you're not saying something, you're sending a message. Thankfully, this powerful statement about communication was the secret to my success. The magic of that message was larger than life for me. It helped me realize I deserved more than feelings of misunderstanding, judgment, and being overlooked. Any thought of playing small in the future came to a screeching halt.

Communication is Everything
What is communication? Some classify the act of communication as a two-way process of sending and receiving messages through verbal and non-verbal means to reach mutual understanding. Others classify the act of communication as the transfer of information from one person to another or the creation and exchange of meaning. I believe the best explanation comes from the person who contributed enormously to the study of human communication and my professor of communication studies, Dr. James McCroskey:

> "Communication is the process of stimulating meaning in the minds of others using verbal or non-verbal messages."

Communication is Everywhere
Communication is how you express yourself including the words you say and don't say, your rate of speech, tone of voice, facial expressions, and body language. It's in text messages, phone calls, family dinners, social gatherings, and business meetings. You communicate through the way you dress, drive, eat, and so much more.

Personally, I believe communication also means freedom: freedom from feeling eclipsed. I believe communication is a prescription for reviving confidence. Through communication, you bring out the best in yourself and others. Communication grants you the ability to build and strengthen relationships. You carry yourself with authority through communication. It provides you with the ability to take charge and reach a level of understanding. You serve as a liaison and make strong connections through communication. You become indispensable and have the ultimate competitive edge. Above all else, know with 100% certainty that communication is the most important skill and the secret to success.

With three degrees in communication, I admit, I'm obsessed with the subject. There's so much to learn and I find the study of communication enormously intriguing. Though not a substitute for a comprehensive study or intended to be a quick fix, below are a few of my communication solutions. They are my beloved Communication Cliff Notes.

> Assume nothing.
> Hug those you love.
> Remove toxic people quickly.
>
> Reasonably timed eye-lock is key.
> Be courageous in what you have to say.
> Know your value and speak your worth.
>
> Seek to understand.
> Make your first impression brilliant.
> A firm handshake is the foundation for trust.
>
> Listen before you speak.
> Feel good about what you are saying and show it.
> Don't take yourself seriously. Loosen up and calm down.

Fresh humor and quick wit wins.
Don't dumb yourself down to build others up.
Facial expressions matter. Smile at life with delight.

Laugh more. Argue less.
Articulate clearly and speak confidently.
Take relationships seriously. Treasure them.

Expiration dates for apologies don't exist.
Refuse to stare, swear, judge, gossip, or gloat.
Folded arms across the chest are rarely a good sign.

Celebrate birthdays.
Timing is everything.
Identify reasons to be happy.

Nurture your passion daily.
Stand tall. Head up. Shoulders back.
Be a door opener. Go out of your way to do this for others.

Communication:
The Most Important Skill & Secret to Success
I knew a person who felt eclipsed. A person that was stuck and suffered from playing small. A person who didn't know their true value or worth. That person used to be me, and possibly, you have felt that way too.

Communication was my path to freedom and success and it will be your as well. It's the foundation for your personal relationships and professional life. It dictates how effective or ineffective you will be in the future. Communication opens the door to an unlimited amount of achievement when you have the skills to speak confidently, seek understanding, and make a lasting impression. Be courageous and communicate clearly your way to success.

Remember: you are, and always will be, your greatest creation.

Jane Richardson, PhD specializes in communication. She distinguishes between effective and ineffective communication, making the complex message clear. In 2003, Jane founded Clearly Communicating, LLC which provides specialized communication solutions for entrepreneurs, private companies, government agencies, and legal communities.

With decades of experience working as a Fortune 500 communication consultant, expert witness, Capitol Hill professional, college teacher, author, and volunteer, Jane had the pleasure of collaborating with many successful organizations including: IBM, U.S. Presidential Campaign, U.S. House of Representatives, Bristol-Meyers Squibb, Ortho-McNeil Pharmaceuticals, St. Jude Children's Research Hospital, Arnold Palmer Spirit of Hope, and Industrial Sales and Manufacturing.

Educated in the U.S. and Europe, Jane has a strong understanding of the communication process including public speaking, persuasion, message analysis and delivery, clarity and comprehension, and verbal and visual coordination.

Jane also co-authored three books that became Number One International Best Sellers including this one, *Rising Above* and

Courageous World Catalysts available at http://amzn.to/2vK4DUm

To find out more about Jane and her communication solutions, please send an email to: jjrcommunication@gmail.com or visit http://www.clearlycommunicating.com/

https://www.linkedin.com/in/janerichardsonphd/

https://twitter.com/4jrich

Nowhere Spells Now Here

By Merav Richter

"You are only free when you realize you belong no place – you belong every place – no place at all.

The price is high. The reward is great."

~ Maya Angelou

It's not often that I get star-struck. Not in that honest to goodness, jaw-on-the-ground, can't put words together because my tongue won't work, and I can't think of a single intelligible thing to say, kind of way.

Not until the day I met Maya Angelou.

In my 23-year career as a flight attendant for a major international airline, I had the chance to meet many, many celebrities, dignitaries, politicians, singers, writers, poets, and all manner and ilk of interesting people. At the beginning of my career, it excited me. I would see them as "other-worldly," somehow graced by some special "celebrity gene" that the rest of us didn't possess. But, as I grew older, and questionably wiser, I saw them as just another person trying to get somewhere.

I looked at starlets up-close and personal and could see that without the professional make-up and hair, they looked just like my neighborhood friends picking up their kids from school. I met big-name movie producers and media moguls who only spoke through their assistants. I met famous authors, activists, athletes, and politicians who treated me and my colleagues as if we were their own personal servants.

I also met many starlets, celebrities and general movers-and-shakers who were as down-to-earth, unpretentious, humble, and kind as you and I are. (Please allow me the presumption that you are all of these things. If you're neither down-to-earth, nor humble, or pretentiously unkind, then humor me for just a minute).

As a professional, whenever I met someone of a reasonable degree of fame, both the humble and not-so-humble variety, I always remained dignified, keeping my equilibrium and class in check.

    Not so, the day I met Maya.

Let me back up and shed some light on the situation.

I only ever wanted to be two things in my life; a flight attendant and a writer. I was under the mistaken assumption (impressed upon me by a highly-strung high-school guidance counselor) that being a flight attendant wasn't a real career, and that writing is a passion one pursues only after finishing university, traveling the world, and gaining some wisdom. My love of writing persisted despite her assuagement, and during my graduation, the Vice-Principal signed my yearbook with "Write On!"

When I was a little girl, I always had my nose in a book and my head in the clouds. The books I read fed my imagination and colored my world with far-off vistas and adventurous women. I danced and sang in my fantasy world, filled with beauty and joyous laughter.

Luckily, choosing to be a flight attendant during my first year of university allowed me to finish my studies, travel the world, and gain much wisdom. It also, gave me the time and freedom to continue writing.

And that passionate writing pursuit brought me to that fortunate day in 2008, when I met my ultimate girl-crush, writing guru, poetess extraordinaire, the Phenomenal Woman herself – Maya Angelou.

She was on a flight from Los Angeles to Toronto. She was low-key and unassuming, sitting in her first-class seat, wearing comfortable pants, a long brown tunic, glasses with lenses that adjusted to the light, yet kept within a shade of dimmed even during the lowered lights of a night flight, and with her trademark head of salt and pepper hair.

I wasn't even quite sure it was her, until she spoke once and smiled twice. Then, she was unmistakably Maya.

It took me many hours to work up the courage to speak with her. What would I say? How should I approach her? What if I bothered her? How should I tell her how much she meant to me? How could I explain the huge impact she had on my life? How could I tell her what an inspiration she was to me? But, then again, how could I _not_?

Finally, as the morning light streamed through the open window shades, I mustered up the bravery to say something. I wasn't articulate. Nor was I intelligent. I probably wasn't even intelligible, but I said what I could.

I told her how much I admired her, aspired to be like her, and how I also wanted to inspire people with my words.

"You already do." She answered, in that wise, sage voice of hers.

I told her how I had always written poetry and the ancient stories of women, how I traveled the world collecting the stories of all the wise, wild, wicked, and wanton women I met, both living and the ones that came before. I told her that when I grew up I wanted to be just like her, that my dream had always been to write, but that I was nowhere near ready.

She turned to face me with that broad, enigmatic smile and said – "Nowhere spells now here."

She told me of her own journey to becoming a writer; as a dancer, a mother, a wanderer, a poet and a free spirit. She told me of her troubled youth, her collection of odd jobs, her persistence at keeping on speaking her truth – even when it was uncomfortable to do so. Even when speaking her truth made her voice shake.

She told me about her writing process – she would rent a hotel room, bring a bottle of her favorite Scotch or Bourbon (depending on what the mood of her writing was), and a pack of cigarettes, or later in life, cigars. She wouldn't emerge until she was done. Even now that she had a beautiful place to write in her home, and all the time to dedicate to her art, she still kept the same structure of writing that she had when she was struggling. She said that the struggle was the secret to her success, to write as if she was still struggling – to remember where she came from.

As the pilot's landing announcement came over the PA, I thanked her for her time, and she reached for my hand and said, "Begin. Now. Here."

That was the day my Sexier Plan was born.

What started as a "six-year plan" until retirement from my corporate job became a Sexier Plan, as I soon came to learn that when you follow your bliss, the universe opens doors for you. And sometimes those doors don't open according to your "plan." They are Sexier.

I realized that day, that I already had everything I needed to begin to follow my dreams. Wishing on a *One Day, Some Day* ideal for when to start my dream only kept me away from actually starting.

I began to earnestly study writing. I attended workshops, read books, worked with mentors, competed in poetry slams, created my morning meditation and writing practice. I wrote everywhere; in journals, on postcards, on napkins, receipts, blogs, articles, post-it notes. I couldn't *not* write anymore.

I started writing in my hotel layovers, sometimes with Scotch and cigarettes, but usually with copious amounts of coffee. The story that I wanted, *needed*, to write since 2001, finally poured through me. By 2012, *The Secret of the Storyteller,* my first novel, was complete.

At the same time, my home life was turning upside-down. The market crashed, my husband lost his job, my sons were going through the preteen angst years, my daughter was diagnosed with autism, and I became the sole income earner for a family of five, with two dogs, a lizard, and a series of unfortunate fish. My Sexier Plan of early retirement, and easing into the full-time writer's life, seemed to be dashed into oblivion.

So, I did what the women in my family always did – I went to work. I worked extra hours, double shifts on the weekends, homeschooled my daughter, made lunches for my sons, walked the dogs, prepared dinner, folded laundry, zipped from one doctor appointment to another, then worked some more.

>I awoke one morning, and I didn't recognize myself.

>Where was that little girl that danced and twirled in the living room?

>The woman who laughed and leaped and loved and lived?

>I was overworked, overweight, overwhelmed, and totally over it.

>I decided to make a change. Actually, I decided to make a huge overhaul.

In the midst of all of that chaos, a door opened. I noticed an ad from my ideal publishing house that was running a spiritual fiction contest. On a whim, I entered *The Secret of the Storyteller* in the contest. I was thrilled when the announcement came a few months later. I, along with a handful of other spiritual authors, had won.

The publisher held a training workshop for all of the emerging authors, teaching us not just the *art* of writing, but also the *craft*. We learned that there is a business model behind success. There are measures, templates and tools. There are frameworks and procedures. There are algorithms, checklists and charts. While these things didn't align with the artist in me, they were the exact structures that I was trained in at my corporate job. Turns out, my corporate job was preparing me for my life as a writer.

In keeping with the instructions of the publishing house, I began to build a platform for my message to the world. I began to write about all the premises in my novel; the divine feminine, women's empowerment, the secrets of the ancient societies, women's archetypes and ecstasy. I created posters and blogs. I got involved in the Women's Movement. I marched and made headlines. I presented and was asked to speak. I was in the right place at the right time. My message went viral and my platform grew. From that place, my second book, *Brave Ecstatic Woman,* was born.

I still flew around the world with the airline, but now, with a much different energy. Before, I felt like I had one foot on a speeding boat, while the other foot was planted firmly on the dock. And I was doing the splits.

Now I realize that it's much easier to leap when you're already dancing. I not only lived my passion of writing, I also got support from the airline. The management loved what I was doing; they even asked me to write for the internal employee magazine.

So, if there is something that you dream of being, doing, or having, that you see others being, doing, or having, just know that it *is* possible to be, do, or have from the exact place you are now. Conversely, if there is something that you simply cannot *not* do – know this – you already do it.

Start now, wherever you are.

Because Nowhere spells Now Here.

Begin. Now. Here.

And you are Here.

Merav Richter is the vivacious hero for brave ecstatic living. Author, career woman, entrepreneur, philosopher, mystic, poet, dancer, traveler, adventurer, comedian... In today's fast-paced, success-driven world, Merav champions a new standard in personal fulfillment – ecstasy!

Through her new book, *Brave Ecstatic Woman*, and her online community of the same name, Merav inspires women around the world to ignite their feminine essence and experience ecstasy in their everyday lives. She is a Best-Selling Author, speaker, and life-long scholar with in-depth knowledge of ancient and modern-day philosophy, mysticism, spirituality, peace training, and the divine feminine.

Through her writing, speaking, and community building, Merav is committed to shifting the paradigms, bridging into a new conscious evolution of humanity, and enjoying the journey.

Brave Ecstatic Woman is her second book. To learn more, visit her at www.MeravRichter.com

The Grit Factor
By Brandi Stephens

The flower that blooms in adversity is the most rare and beautiful of all.

~ The Emperor of China from **Mulan**

My life has always been guided by a common theme -- keeping going; do not quit. I am the oldest of four children, and I was required to be responsible, not just for myself, but for my siblings as well, at a very early age. My parents focused primarily on their desires rather than on what was best for the family. My stepfather chased money to fulfill his wants, while my mother was a stay-at-home mom. I can recall numerous times that the electricity was shut off or we didn't have any food in the refrigerator, but my parents still went out to dinner without us. I attended 13 different schools before the ninth grade because we moved around so much due to evictions. There was an expectation for me to be responsible for my siblings, but I also felt as though I had to care for them because of our situation. It was a very difficult experience to go through as a child and teenager, but I knew that my life would be better. I said to myself, "When you get out on your own, do something with yourself so you don't have to come back to this." I had to be an example for my siblings so that they could have a stable life as well. The ability to hang out with friends after school or go to the movies on the weekends was non-existent for me. I honestly did not feel it was fair for me to have to take on the responsibility of raising my sisters and brother. I love them dearly, but I feel like I missed so much of my childhood. Yet, I do not have any regrets because that experience made me into the woman I am today. I learned responsibility at a very early age and understand the importance of sacrifice and prioritizing wants and necessities.

One of the ways I often used to escape the day-to-day job of being a second mother to my siblings was to become extremely focused on school. This focus worked well for me because I excelled in my schoolwork, and I was able to break away from some of the domestic tasks to do homework, study for tests, and daydream about how my life would be when I went off to college. I truly enjoyed school and was eager to learn. Although many teens may not have been able to handle the pressure of looking after three kids, cooking, cleaning, and keeping up with school work, my childhood taught me to keep going, even when life was hard.

My life took a dramatic shift in 2003, around the time of my high school graduation. As with most students, the months and weeks leading up to my graduation were some of the best days ever. I was so excited and proud of myself for graduating. I'd maintained a high GPA throughout all four years of my high school experience, and I had my mind set and application completed for the university that was my dream school to attend. As I was getting measured for my cap and gown, my guidance counselor asked me to come to her office before I left the campus for the day. When I walked into her office, she seemed very upset. She looked at me and said that she received phone calls from the universities I applied to, and they asked her to verify that I was who I claimed to be. I was confused as to why the colleges needed to call to verify my identity. My guidance counselor informed me that my name and my social security number did not match up. I had no idea what was going on, and I resolved that I would get to the bottom of the issue.

Once I left the guidance counselor's office, I immediately called my mother and explained the situation to her. My mother didn't seem shocked at all and stated that we would talk about it later. That evening, my parents took me to dinner. While in the car on the way to the restaurant, my father told me that he isn't my biological father and my last name, which was the same as his, was not my legal name. My entire world shifted in the matter of a moment. I realized I couldn't attend my dream school, and I learned that the people that I trusted the most had lied to me for years. I was so confused, scared, and angry. I honestly believed that my life and plans were ruined.

It was definitely not an easy road to recovery. I was determined to complete my dream of graduating college and I did just that. But, I had to start at square one, I enrolled at a local state college but did not do well my first year, due to the stress and drama caused by my paternity situation. I did not receive financial assistance from my parents at all. Therefore, I decided to take time away from school to work full-time and support myself. Even though I did not want to leave school, I knew I had to work to survive. I was determined to finish my education. I worked for almost five years after graduating high school, so I was able to go back to college and complete my education. I did not allow the fact that I did not have support from my parents prevent me from accomplishing my goal of obtaining my degree. There was a period of a few years that I did not have much contact with my family. I was angry over the situation, and I did not want that anger to be a distraction from achieving my goal. That experience taught me many lessons about perseverance, and it allowed me to know that I can accomplish and attain anything that I desire with focus and determination. Little did I know, that learning that my step-father was not my biological father, would not be the biggest life crisis that I would have to face.

In the summer of 2011, I learned that I was expecting my first child. My husband and I were excited and nervous all at the same time. It seemed as if pregnancy brought an additional layer of happiness into our lives. I read books about what kind of diet to have while pregnant, which products to avoid, the best positions to sleep in, etc. I wanted to be sure that I did everything in my ability to bring forth a healthy baby. At 5 ½ months pregnant, I woke up in the middle of the night to pain in my back and was not sure why. My husband rushed me to the hospital and we learned that I, in fact, was in labor. I never thought I could go into labor so early, and pleaded with the doctor, "I'm not full-term. How can we stop it?" I was in shock and felt so unprepared for what was taking place. She told me that we didn't have any control in this matter, and that my body had already started to dilate. I was again faced with a situation that totally shifted my life in the matter of moments. Our beautiful baby girl was born at 5 ½ months and lived for only a brief time after her birth. At that moment, I truly realized how precious and fragile life can be.

Losing my first child had such a significant impact on my personality and my social interactions. I did not want to do anything or go anywhere during my time of healing. I did not know that my heart could ache so much. I cried for weeks, and I was so depressed. I prayed and asked God to please take away the emptiness that I felt and to bring my joy back. I knew that joy was on the other side of my healing, so I took time to care for myself. I made an effort to do my hair and makeup, to get out of the house, and to talk with a grief counselor. I began to be grateful for the entire experience because I wanted to honor my baby girl's life no matter how brief it was. I learned that lying down in my pain did not serve my purpose in life. I forced myself to get back to living my life and loving it.

The time came when I was strong enough mentally and physically to try again for another child. I desperately wanted to bless my husband, who really wanted a baby. We discovered that we were pregnant again, but because of our first experience, we decided not to say anything until I was at least six months pregnant. I anxiously counted the days until I made it to 24 weeks -- six months. I was so happy and relieved on that day. We decided to let our immediate family know about the pregnancy, and they were also elated.

Then, in my 25 ½ week I began to have the same back pain that I had with the first pregnancy. My husband immediately rushed me to the hospital and we were informed that once again, I was in labor. I was rushed to the OR for an emergency C-Section. Our son was hurried to the NICU just seconds after his birth. My husband and I became NICU parents, which was an emotional rollercoaster. Seeing our son connected to tubes and monitors was an experience that I would not wish on my worst enemy. My husband was unable to get time off work during these weeks so it was a lonely time for us both. We were blessed to stay at the Ronald McDonald house which was on the hospital property and made it very convenient for us to quickly get to the hospital.

Five weeks later, our son left this earth and met his older sister. I thought I was going to literally lose my mind. I had the same feelings I had with my first loss, yet it was intensified 100 times. I could not believe what was happening. I blamed myself; I felt like less of a woman. I believed that my husband and I should go our separate ways, because this was the second baby that I lost. That experience was one of the most difficult situations that I ever had to grow through.

A few years passed, and I desired to try again for another baby. I was told by many doctors that I would always go into labor in my second trimester due to a condition they found after my son was born. They informed me that there was nothing that they could do to help me deliver a child within my third trimester of pregnancy. Even some of our family and friends insisted that we should not try again. But, I desired to be a mom, and I did not care about what people said or thought about me. So, through counseling, prayer, and finding a great OB/GYN, our miracle baby was born. I had an awesome team of physicians who understood my issue, and they created a plan to ensure that I delivered a healthy baby. Our son is now two-years old and I am so grateful to be his mother. If I had given up on having children after my second loss, I would have never been able to experience the love and wonderful joy of being a mother. It is so important to keep running after your goals and dreams even after failure. Do not allow failure to keep you from achieving your heart's desire. Keep going. Do not quit.

Everyone on this earth is capable of triumphing over his or her tragedies. It does not matter how far you think you are from the finish line, you better believe you have the capacity to handle anything that life throws at you. The key is to keep moving forward and to stay focused on the goal and the desire. Even in situations when you think you've lost, don't give up. Keep going. Use the fear, use the pain, use the naysayers as fuel to get you to your destination of success.

I hope my story has encouraged you in such a way to get you to your next level of greatness. I believe in you, and I wish you all the best. I live by these words every day. I remind myself that I can have anything that I choose to believe. I have gone through many painful situations in life, but they have all made me stronger, so I can reach the next level and live my best life.

Brandi Stephens is a Life/Resilience Coach who is inspired to primarily help women see the beauty in their pain and to reach their fullest potential on their journey back to wholeness. Brandi was born and raised in Southern California, but now lives in Illinois and likes spending time with her family and mentoring young women. She recently transitioned to a career in education to fulfill her dream of becoming an educator. Her previous career as an HR professional allowed her the opportunity to assist many individuals with their career journeys. Brandi has learned to live a life of gratitude and to be present in the moment.

Brandi can be contacted at: stephens.brandi@icloud.com

Or on Instagram at: iambrandistephens.

It's Time to Take That Leap With FAITH!

By Beverly Walthour

Being an entrepreneur is NOT for everyone. There I said it. In a world where it seems as if EVERYONE in the online world is making $10K a month overnight, flying on private jets, and drinking mimosas on the beach every morning, it appears as if being an entrepreneur is easy-peasy. If that is what you believe, then I seriously ask you to reconsider your reasons for becoming an entrepreneur. There are going to be 12-hour days, technology that crashes in the middle of your presentation, clients that decide not to work with you further, and deals that fall through at the last minute. How you handle those tough times will determine your success as an entrepreneur. Your WHY must be crystal-clear and enough to support you when you don't see any other way. This process includes getting outside your comfort zone and taking leaps with FAITH when things start to get comfortable.

As a Business Strategist for Christian female coaches, women come to me daily with a desire to create the time and financial freedom they see displayed so casually on social media. They are frustrated and beginning to doubt if they should continue in their business, because they are not seeing the same results that others have. They start to ask themselves, "What is wrong with me?" I remind them that if GOD placed this business on their heart, then they should continue moving forward. However, I remind them to take their focus off what others are doing in their businesses, and really focus on their own 'why' for starting their business. When they accomplish these two steps, they will not be so easily swayed by what they see and hear around them.

My 'why' has always been so much bigger than me. I know I was put on this earth to impact the globe. At first, I wanted to impact my family by being the first person to go to college. I knew that if I wanted a better life, I had to get a college education. Being a college graduate allowed me to show my family and myself that there were other options outside of going straight into the workforce or into the military. Holding on to my 'why' got me through being away from home for four years, maintaining the HOPE scholarship, and navigating the social landscape of college. Although I did not always know my next step, my WHY kept me moving forward.

After four years of college, I graduated with honors from the University of Georgia with a BS in Middle School Education. Although I knew I would not retire as an educator, I set off to change lives. With my degree, my desire to impact my family shifted to a determination to impact my community. Not only did I want my middle-school students to be successful in the classroom, but I also wanted them to be successful in life. Although I was a great classroom teacher, was named Teacher of the Year, and served in a number of leadership positions, I began to feel that something was missing.

It took me about a year to figure out what was wrong. I thought back to the fact that I always knew that I would not retire from the field of education. So, in 2007, I boldly took a leap with FAITH and left my career of seven years to start a K-12 in-home tutoring company. I left the comfort of everything I knew to venture out into the unknown. When I taught school, I knew what time be at work, what I was going to teach

each class period, how much I was going to be paid each month, and when I was going on vacation. However, as an entrepreneur, that comfort was no longer there. As a new entrepreneur, I worked longer hours, trying to find clients so that I could pay my bills, and was unsure about what each day would bring.

Unfortunately, I did not prepare myself for the shift from being an employee to being an entrepreneur. Although I was able to get clients and even hired other tutors to work with me, I let fear of the unknown overpower my thinking. Due to this fear, I started asking questions like, "What if I don't get more clients?" "What if I fail as an entrepreneur?" "What if I can't pay my mortgage?" Eventually, that fear won out, and I went back into the classroom. At least there, I knew exactly what was going to happen each day. So, I went back to my comfort zone.

However, I had been bitten by the entrepreneurial bug, and I couldn't shake it. Although my first business did not work out the way I planned, I loved having freedom with my time and determining how much I could make each month. So, during the seven years back in the classroom, I also started two multi-level marketing companies on the side. By the end of that period, I knew I was no longer called to teach. The desire to have a bigger impact gnawed at me hard. So, for the second time, I resigned from my teaching job to start a new career. I became a trainer for educators in the state of Georgia. I absolutely loved what I did, and I was able to have a bigger impact by working with educators all over the state. However, six months later, the position for which I was hired was eliminated, and I was laid off. That loss was a huge blow to me. I said to GOD, "I know you did not have me leave a career of 14 years to be laid off six months later." Right then and there, I made a vow never to rely solely on another company for my income. I knew I had to start my own business again. During this time, I was with the multi-level marketing companies, but I needed work where I received more than a percentage of the revenue for all my hard work.

Although I was able to find another training job with an educational software company within the next month, being laid off from my previous job changed the course of my life. Around this time, people started asking me how I was able to start so many businesses. I began offering them advice on what I did to start my businesses. After a while, I realized there was a need for services to help others start their own businesses. My 10 years as an entrepreneur, plus my 15 years as an educator and trainer made me an excellent fit as a Business Strategist. Not only did I know how to start and make money in a business, but I also knew how people learned and processed information. That's when my coaching business, BCW Business Ventures, LLC, was born. My 'why' for starting my business was not only so that I could create a global impact by helping other female entrepreneurs start profitable online businesses, but also so that I could create the time and financial freedom that having a typical job could not give me.

When I launched my coaching business, I still also worked as a trainer. In full transparency, this job was my safety net, and initially it caused me to not commit 100% to my coaching business. I knew that if there was a month I did not hit my financial goal in my business, it was okay because I had the income from my job as a trainer to fall back on. But GOD always has a way of shaking things up for me.

About six months after starting my coaching business, my young niece and nephew came to live with me for a while, even though I was a single woman with no kids. During that time, not only did I travel one to six days a week for my job, but I also tried to grow my coaching business on the side. On my travel days, the kids stayed with the babysitter. One day, my niece said to me, "Auntie Bev, you are always gone." Her statement hit me like a ton of bricks. They came to live with me for stability, and here I was shuffling them off to the babysitter every week. It was then and there that I had to make a decision. Now, I had two little people relying on me, so my WHY for starting my business became so much bigger. Before, I wanted to have a global impact and to create time and financial freedom. Now, my 'why' also involved impacting my family again. So, taking another leap with FAITH, I put in my two weeks' notice at my training job. This leap was bigger than before, because it impacted the lives of my niece and nephew too! I knew this time around, I had to make my coaching business work.

As I got more and more involved in my coaching business, I realized that there were pieces in my business that were out of alignment with who I was. I began to feel a tug that my client base was too broad for effective results. When I analyzed who I helped get the best results, they were coaches and consultants. And when I really looked at that group even more closely, I realized the women I attracted were Christians. Initially, I hesitated to narrow down my client base. I came up with all kinds of excuses: I would have to change my bio on my social media pages, I would have to update my website, etc. However, at that same time, I came across an amazing copywriter and my web designer was already working with me on my site. So, the "reasons" I had for not wanting to narrow down my client base were quickly eliminated. In other words, GOD made sure to remove any reason for me not to move forward with marketing to my new client base.

I did get some pushback from people about the group that I served in my business, but overall, the support has been overwhelming. Some of that opposition included people who felt that I would have a bigger impact if I served those people that did not know Christ. However, I truly believe this is the group I am supposed to support in their coaching businesses. I show them that Christian coaches can have financial success without compromising their beliefs. I absolutely love the fact that I get to partner with women who know that they are on this earth for a bigger purpose, and they all desire to have a global impact and change the world!

When these women come to me, they are ready to do the work it takes to create this impact. On a daily basis, they make a vow to get outside their comfort zones, invest time and money, and do the work necessary to create successful coaching businesses. Because of this, my clients experience amazing results, not only in their businesses, but in their lives as well. Yes, they are able to generate clients and income, but the biggest part is that they are able to create that impact they desire! So many of them see their coaching business as a means to a bigger end; it is a stepping stone to starting their own schools, community centers, and platforms that enable other women to grow and prosper.

Since I have been obedient to my calling, amazing opportunities have been presented to me. One of the biggest chances that opened for me was to host my own TV and radio shows in Atlanta, GA. Through these opportunities, I can provide my clients with a platform to have their 'why' seen and heard by hundreds of thousands of other people. All these opportune circumstances happened because I decided to take that leap with FAITH and to not let fear control what I do anymore.

As I look back at my 'why,' I realize that it has changed. It began as the desire to impact my family when I went off to college. It then morphed into the urge to impact my community as an educator. Now, I am able to have a global impact as a Business Strategist. I get to show women around the globe that they can live the life they desire if they want to. They can use their businesses to have an impact that affects the globe, if that is what they desire. I show them this possibility through my coaching, workshops, and speaking engagements. I want them to see through my experiences, that they can have everything they desire in their lives and businesses, but they must be willing to take that leap with FAITH!

Being an entrepreneur is definitely not for everyone. There will be many peaks and valleys. Things do not always go as planned, and you must be willing to stick it out for the long haul if you want to have longevity. The key to this process is getting outside your comfort zone by taking those leaps of FAITH and trusting that you will get what you want, or maybe, even something better. By making decisions from the perspective of the person I desire to be versus the person that

I currently see in front of me, I am able to take those leaps. So now, my question to you is, are YOU ready to take your next leap with FAITH?

Beverly Walthour is a Business Strategist for Christian female coaches. She shows them how to create consistent clients and income in 12 weeks or less. She has more than 15 years of experience as an award-winning educator, speaker, consultant, and trainer and over 10 years as an entrepreneur.

Beverly Walthour is the host of the *Talking Business with Beverly* TV show and the host of the *Talking Business with Beverly* Morning Radio Show. She is also the published co-author of the book, *Tying the Knot Between Ministry and the Marketplace, Vol. 1 & 2*. She has been featured in numerous magazines, blogs, television and radio programs, and podcasts. She works with her clients one-on-one, in group programs, and through intensives, online courses, and in-person workshops. She resides in the Atlanta, Georgia area and enjoys spending time with friends and family.

To schedule a call to see how Beverly can support you in creating consistent clients and income in your coaching or consulting business, apply here: bit.ly/beverlycall2018

Website: http://beverlywalthour.com/

Email: beverly@beverlywalthour.com

You can find her on Facebook, Instagram, Twitter, Pinterest, YouTube, and LinkedIn @beverlywalthour

Now that you've read these amazing stories, how would you like to be part of the next anthology project and spread your message worldwide?

All you have to do is turn in your story and I'm going to give you easy-to-follow steps to writing it so that it speaks to those people who need your help. I'm also going to take away the tech overwhelm by publishing the book for you and guaranteeing the Best Seller status. Plus, I'm even going to have your story edited by my team.

➔ **Go here for details on the next project** – join or get on the waiting list: http://bit.ly/nextanthology

* * * * * * * * * * * * * *

What's it like being in an anthology like this one?

Just see what the co-authors of this book say …..

I love working with Vickie, both as my personal coach and with the anthology. I feel so much potential working with her. She really helps me to see my greatness. Being part of the anthology is amazing because it is inspiring 1000's of people to step into their purpose. Its important that we step forward and show by example that it wasn't all easy, but if we can do it, so can you! Vickie is also such a lovely and authentic woman. I recommend her all the time!

~ Jay Diamond, Pleasure and Intimacy Coach, Best Selling Author, Speaker

* * * * * * *

I have always loved to create and share stories, especially those with a Little Lesson of Life that can inspire others in their journey. I have never thought of myself as a writer, and publishing a book was not something I would have ever pursed on my own. Vickie Gould changed this for me and opened the path for me to share my hidden treasures with the world.

I have now published two books with Vickie's assistance and it has been a simple and rewarding journey each time. Now is your time. Write your stories and Vickie will walk the journey of publishing with you. I plan to share so much more with the world and I know I can because of Vickie.

~ *Brooks Gibbs,* Author & Mentor

* * * * * * *

A dream to me published can true when I joined the Anthology. You can say that I "rose above" a belief that it should be difficult and complicated. It was instead an easy, supportive and inspiring experience.

~ *Laverne Wyatt,*

* * * * * * *

➔ **Go here for details on the next project** – join or get on the waiting list: http://bit.ly/nextanthology

I can't wait to meet you!